SPIRITUAL CAPITAL

SPIRITUAL
CAPITAL

Wealth We Can Live By

DANAH ZOHAR
IAN MARSHALL

BLOOMSBURY

First published in Great Britain 2004
This paperback edition published 2005

Copyright © 2004 by Danah Zohar and Ian Marshall

The moral right of the authors has been asserted

Bloomsbury Publishing Plc, 36 Soho Square, London W1D 3QY

A CIP catalogue record for this book is available from the British Library

ISBN 0 7475 7048 5
9780747570486

10 9 8 7 6 5 4 3 2 1

Printed by Clays Ltd, St Ives plc

All papers used by Bloomsbury Publishing are natural,
recyclable products made from wood grown in well-managed forests.
The manufacturing processes conform to the
environmental regulations of the country of origin.

www.bloomsbury.com/danahzohar

For Mats Lederhausen and Michael Rennie—
May others follow their lead.

Contents

Preface

I wrote this book for very personal reasons. When my son was five, he asked me one night at bedtime why he had a life. It took me several weeks at that time to tell him he should live his life to leave the world a better place than he had found it. That was a weighty thought for a five-year-old. But when he reached his late teens, the same question came up again, this time in the context of wondering whether to go to university, what to study, and what career to follow. I found myself giving him much the same answer, that whatever path he chose to follow, he should lead a life that makes a difference. As happens between parents and children, I found that my advice to my son made me call myself to account. Was I using my own life to best advantage?

This self-questioning came at a low point in my life. For perhaps the past two years I had fallen into quite a deep depression about the conduct of some individual people and about the state of our Western culture in general. I had experienced some personal betrayals, been on the receiving end of some stupidity, thoughtlessness, or violence, or seen these things inflicted on others—members of my family, friends, people whose stories were told daily on the television news.

At the same time, I became quite gloomy about the lack of deep values and "intelligent" thought in many sectors of our society. When I spoke at business conferences or gave in-house presentations in the corporate world about features of human intelligence that might generate goodness, creativity, vision, and less stress, all people wanted to know was how they could use this intelligence to make more money on Monday morning. This corporate attitude seemed to reflect the greed and materialism that dog our wider culture. All too often, I felt, we wealthy Western people act from lower motivations like greed, anger, and self-assertion at the expense of our own quality of life. All in all, I felt we live much of our lives in a spiritual desert distinguished by superficiality, absence of commitment, and lack of deep meaning. I experienced this as a victim, helpless to do anything about it.

Talking to my son about his future threw all this gloom into a new perspective. If I was advising him to use his life to make a difference, how could I justify letting myself feel so helpless to do so? I came out of my stultifying depression and began to think. I reread some books that had once inspired me, and came across this passage by Carl Jung, the distinguished analyst who took psychology beyond Freudian gloom.

> If things go wrong in the world, this is
> because something is wrong with the
> individual, because something is wrong
> with me. Therefore, if I am sensible, I shall
> put myself right first. . . . In the last

> analysis, the essential thing is the life of the
> individual. This alone makes history, here
> alone do the great transformations just take
> place, and the whole future, the whole
> history of the world, ultimately spring as a
> gigantic summation from these hidden
> sources in individuals. In our most private
> and most subjective lives we are not only
> the passive witnesses of our age, its
> sufferers, but also its makers. We make our
> own epoch.[1]

"It is in our own most private and subjective lives
that we make the epoch." Those words inspired this
book. They underpin its central theme, that if enough of
us change ourselves, we can thereby change the world. I
began the task on myself by putting aside my gloomy
inactivity and its associated avoidance mechanisms and
getting myself back into in a state to write.

Human beings have a tremendous range of potential,
from the very worst we can imagine to heights of sublim-
ity. All too often, most of us slob around somewhere just
below the mean point on this scale. We allow ourselves
to be controlled by lower motivations like greed and
anger; we hurt others and ourselves. Sometimes this is
because we make bad choices in life, but most of us
would seldom actively choose to do wrong or to hurt
others. As Ogden Nash once wrote:[2]

> How could anybody corner wheat
> If he ever stopped to think that thereby he was making a
> lot of people unable to afford to eat.

The trouble is that most of us don't think. We just
avoid choice and let things unfold, content to go
through our lives as sleepwalkers, or as bits of flotsam

in the stream of events. In the course of this we allow a lot of harm to be done and leave a lot of good undone. We avert our glance when we see someone in trouble, we let others take the blame for things we have done, we don't confront painful truths about ourselves, our motives, and our actions, or we exclude whole groups of people from the arena of our moral concern. Yet this avoidance of choice is a deeper denial of our humanity than actively to choose the bad. Our humanity is defined by our ability to choose between right and wrong. Not to choose at all is to deny this essence.

Writing this book has been a personal call to arms for me. It is written for individuals in all walks of our society who are willing to let their lives make a difference. The book was written during difficult times for the world. It was sometimes hard to continue, but family and friends convinced me it is neither naive nor utopian to believe that our world could be a better place. It is we who must make it so.

The book has been drawn from a fourfold knowledge base:

- My personal life experience
- Ideas from the "new science," particularly quantum physics, chaos and complexity science
- My ten years' personal experience as a management educator and consultant
- My general observations of the world, shared with colleagues and friends

Acknowledgments

I want to thank Mats Lederhausen and Michael Rennie for allowing me to use their personal stories. The questions used in Chapter Nine as behavioral and cultural indicators of high SQ were drafted largely by Peter Saul, of Sydney, Australia. I would like to thank Peter for allowing me to use them, and Sandra Cormack at Macquarie University Graduate School of Management for enabling us to collaborate. Finally, I would like to express gratitude to our beloved friend Emilios Bouratinos for his contributions to the dialogues that underpin this book.

The book is written in the first person, using the voice of Danah Zohar. But most ideas in the book represent the joint thinking of both authors. The "Scale of Motivations" is entirely the work of Ian Marshall. The two authors are partners in marriage and in work, and generate ideas together through constant dialogue.

Danah Zohar
Ian Marshall
Oxford, England
January 2004

Introduction

Changing Ourselves to Change the World

Recently, while visiting Nepal, I had a dream that bears on the theme and unfolding of this book. In the dream I was attending a play with three acts, at a theater-in-the-round where the audience sit very close to the actors and feel part of the action. In Act One of the play, a group of Tibetan monks were chanting their prayers and performing the rituals of Tibetan Buddhism. The scene was very ordered, beautiful and peaceful and uplifting to watch. Everything was in its place. But then suddenly the wooden-beamed ceiling of the room began to collapse. Poles and plaster began to rain down on the monks and killed many of them. I ran from the stage in fear for my own life.

In Act Two of the play, Tibetan monks were again performing rituals, but they were old men, bitter and cynical. They were just going through their ceremonies as a matter of habit and appearance, and they were behaving cruelly, even sadistically, to the younger novice monks who attended them. This act of the play had no life. Indeed it was filled with very negative energy and I wanted to flee the theater.

In Act Three of the play, a group of very young novice monks were setting off on a journey. Some were walking, others riding yaks (long-haired, bull-like creatures). These monks were innocent, even naive. They were not certain of their goal, but they knew it was their destiny to travel and discover new rituals for their order. As in all the best dreams, they were riding off into a rising sun, filled with hope and a sense of adventure.

I found the dream an uncanny representation of how our own culture has unfolded. The peaceful monks of Act One, performing their healthy rituals, represented a more traditional time, with "God in his heaven and all right with the world." It was a time of belief and values, a time when human beings knew where the goal posts were. The cynical monks of Act Two represented our modern era, dominated by capitalist materialism and bleak Newtonian mechanics. Theirs (ours) was a world of disillusion, bitterness, selfishness, and even perversion. It was (is) a world where people just go through the motions of once-meaningful things. No one was nourished. The young monks of Act Three, I would like to think, are where at least some of us are today, setting out on a journey to discover new, living rituals (practices, philosophies) that can take our race forward into a meaningful and sustainable future.

I very much hope that a critical mass of individuals can identify with the young monks of Act Three, finding new and broader foundations for our capitalist ethos and our business culture that will use to the full their potential both as material-wealth-generating mechanisms and as fuller human activities. Perhaps a few will find inspiration in the pages that follow.

It is the assumption of this book that our capitalist culture and the business practices that operate within it are in crisis. I describe global business as "a monster consuming itself." This is because the underlying ethos and assumptions of capitalism, and many of the business practices that follow from them, are unsustainable. Capitalism and business as we know them have no long-term future, and these limit the future of our culture at large.

The central theme of this book is that a critical mass of individuals acting from higher motivations can make a difference. Its purpose is to show how this critical mass of present and potential leaders can use their spiritual intelligence to create spiritual capital in their wider organizational cultures, thereby making those cultures more sustainable. The goal is a capitalism that is itself sustainable and a world in which sustainable capitalism can generate wealth that nourishes all our human needs.

The key word here is *wealth*. My own definition of wealth is "that which we have access to that enhances the quality of life." We often speak of a wealth of talent, a wealth of character, or a wealth of good fortune. The word wealth itself comes from the Old English *welth,* meaning "to be well." But the dictionary definition of wealth, reflecting the economized culture that has produced our modern dictionaries, emphasizes first, "a great quantity or store of money." Our usual definition of capital follows from this, defining capital as the amount of money or material goods that we possess. Capitalism as we know it is about money and material wealth.

Spiritual capital, by contrast, is wealth that we can live by, wealth that enriches the deeper aspects of our lives. It is wealth we gain through drawing upon our deepest meanings, deepest values, most fundamental purposes, and highest motivations, and by finding a way to embed these in our lives and work.

Spiritual capital is a vision and a model for organizational and cultural sustainability within a wider framework of community and global concern. It is capital amassed through serving, in both corporate philosophy and practice, the deeper concerns of humanity and the planet. It is capital that reflects our shared values, shared visions, and fundamental purposes in life. Spiritual capital is reflected in what an organization believes in, what it exists for, what it aspires to, and what it takes responsibility for.

My use of the word *spiritual* here and throughout the book has no connection with religion or any other organized belief system. Religious organizations and religiously based cultures have undoubtedly built some genuine spiritual capital. But they have done so within the limitations of belief systems that exclude those who hold other religious beliefs and those who have no religious belief. The broader kind of spiritual capital needed for organizations, communities, and cultures participating in today's pluralist and global society must draw on deeper, nonsectarian meanings, values, purposes, and motivations that might be sacred to any human being.

In the same spirit as this broader spiritual capital, spiritual intelligence is the intelligence with which we access our deepest meanings, values, purposes, and highest motivations. It is how we use these in our thinking processes, in the decisions that we make, and the things that we think it is worthwhile to do. These decisions include how we make and how we allocate our material wealth.

Spiritual intelligence is our moral intelligence, giving us an innate ability to distinguish right from wrong. It is the intelligence with which we exercise goodness, truth, beauty, and compassion in our lives. It is, if you like, the soul's intelligence, if you think of *soul* as that channeling capacity in human beings that brings things up from the deeper and richer dimensions of imagination and spirit into our daily lives, families, organizations, and institutions.

To understand the book, it is necessary to see the crucial link between spiritual intelligence, spiritual capital, and sustainability. This link is the central unifying thread running through the book. It can be expressed as follows: *We need a sense of meaning and values and a sense of fundamental purpose (spiritual intelligence) in order to build the wealth that these can generate (spiritual capital).* It is only when our notion of capitalism includes spiritual capital's wealth of meaning, values, purpose, and higher motivation that we can have sustainable capitalism and a sustainable society.

> Spiritual intelligence is the intelligence with which we access our deepest meanings, values, purposes, and highest motivations.
>
> SQ, spiritual capital, and sustainability are crucially linked. SQ's sense of meaning, values, and purpose generates spiritual capital. Spiritual capital's wealth of meaning, values, and higher motivation are necessary to sustainable capitalism and a sustainable society.

Sustainability itself requires that a system be able to maintain itself and evolve into the future. Sustainable systems in nature are systems whose elements cooperate in producing a balanced environment that nourishes the whole. They are holistic (the parts interact internally), self-organizing, and exploratory. The earth's ecology (Gaia) is an example, where plants produce the oxygen that animals need, animals in turn produce carbon dioxide needed by the plants, the various plant and animal populations stay in balance through a combination of cooperation and competition, and water is recycled through processes of evaporation and rain. The ecology as a whole uses the diversity within it to breed evolution (genetic mutation).

People, organizations, and cultures that have spiritual capital will be more sustainable because they will have developed qualities that include wider, values-based vision, global concern and compassion, long-term thinking, spontaneity (and hence flexibility), an ability to act from their own deepest convictions, an ability to thrive on diversity, and an ability to learn from and make positive use of adversity.

I discuss three kinds of capital in the book: material capital, social capital, and spiritual capital. The building of each kind of capital is, I believe, associated with one of our three major human intelligences: rational intelligence (IQ), emotional intelligence (EQ), and spiritual intelligence (SQ).

Capital	Intelligence	Function
Material Capital	IQ: Rational Intelligence	What I think
Social Capital	EQ: Emotional Intelligence	What I feel
Spiritual Capital	SQ: Spiritual Intelligence	What I am

Material capital is the capital most familiar to us in our present capitalist society. It means money and the things that money can buy—money to spend, money to invest, money with which to buy material advantage, power, and influence. As the founders of capitalism maintained, we pursue this kind of capital with our rational intelligence (IQ). IQ is the intelligence with which we think.

Social capital is the wealth that makes our communities and organizations function effectively for the common good. Francis Fukuyama defines social capital as the ability of people to work together for common purposes in groups and organizations. He argues that this is an ability that arises from trust and from shared ethical values.[1] Social capital is reflected in the kinds of relationships we build in our families, communities, and organizations, the amount we trust one another, the extent to which we fulfill our responsibilities to one another and the community, the amounts of health and literacy we achieve through our common efforts, and the extent to which we are free of crime.

The amassing of social capital depends largely on the amount of emotional intelligence we can bring to our relationships. Emotional intelligence is our ability to understand and feel for other people, our ability to read other people's emotions or to read the social situations we are in, and to behave or respond appropriately. EQ is the intelligence with which we feel.

Spiritual capital, as noted, adds the dimension of our shared meanings and values and ultimate purposes. It addresses those concerns we have about what it means to be human and the ultimate meaning and purpose of human life. I strongly believe that really genuine social capital must include this spiritual dimension. It is the cultivation and sharing of our truly ultimate concerns that acts as the real glue of society. Spiritual capital is built by using our spiritual intelligence. SQ is the intelligence with which we *are*.

All three kinds of capital—material, social, and spiritual—must be built, using all three of our intelligences, if we are to have sustainable capitalism. My emphasis in this book is on building the spiritual capital component of that whole equation. *No other kind of capital really works without an underlying base of spiritual capital.*

Motivation, the kinds of motivation we experience and the possibility of shifting from behavior inspired by lower motivations to that inspired by higher motivations, is a strong subtheme of the book. It is only when we know what underlying motives are driving our negative and self-destructive behavior that we can aspire to acting from higher motivations. The twelve dynamic processes of our spiritual intelligence provide an energy input that enables us to shift our individual behavior. My point, then, is that a critical mass of individuals, using their spiritual intelligence to act from higher motivations, can shift the dominant features of a whole culture, be it that of a family, a community, an organization, or of a whole global culture like capitalism.

The motivational transformation of individuals and cultures in all aspects of society is critical if we really are to build a better world, and those who live and work within such diverse areas of life as education, psychology, politics, the professions, and business can benefit from amassing spiritual capital, and thus from reading this book. Indeed, it is crucial we get them all on board. But I have chosen business as the audience from which I have drawn most of my examples and to which I address most of my remarks in the book. I have two reasons for this choice. First, business is the dominant instrument through which capitalist values have permeated our society. If we want to broaden the values of capitalism, it must be done, hands on, by broadening the values of a significant number of businesspeople. Second, it is business today that has the money and the power to make a very significant difference in the way that wealth of all kinds is generated and used to benefit individuals and society at large.

For business to be in a position to make such a difference, though, business culture must make a significant shift. This shift can only come about if the senior leadership of business act to change themselves. The book envisages the creation of a critical mass of business leaders (current and potential) who would act from higher motivations. I call this critical mass *knights*. Like the monks in my Tibetan dream, these men and women will have the creativity and the motivation to invent and embody new, living practices and a philosophy of business that can take us into a meaningful and sustainable future.

The book makes many criticisms of capitalism and of business-as-usual. Chapter One is a catalogue of wrongs and problems, many of them already familiar to the sophisticated reader. But the book is not anti-capitalist or anti-business. The anti-capitalists are wrong to reject an economic mechanism that has generated more material wealth than mankind has ever known. The trick is not to reject capitalism but to transform it. I see a rich potential within business and other fields to generate, within a wider framework, even more wealth and value, some of which can be used for the common good of humanity.

What follows is a "fractal" book. It is addressed, simultaneously, to the level of the individual and to the societal and cultural levels. Each level mirrors the others, and the same dynamic principles apply on each level.

The book's development follows its main theme of how a critical mass of individuals, acting from higher motivations, can change the world. Chapters One and

Two describe the two very different scenarios of capitalism in business-as-we-know-it, and capitalism in business-as-it-could-be. The first scenario portrays a materialist, amoral (often immoral) culture of short-term self-interest, profit maximization, emphasis on shareholder value, isolationist thinking, and profligate disregard of its own long-term consequences. It is based on narrow assumptions about human nature and motivation. The second scenario is that of spiritual capital. This portrays a values-based capitalist and business culture in which wealth is accumulated to generate a decent profit while acting to raise the common good. Its emphasis is more on "stakeholder value," where stakeholders include the whole human race, present and future, and the planet itself. Spiritual capital nourishes and sustains the human spirit as well as making business sustainable.

The rest of the book is devoted to the process of how we can actually shift from today's scenario to that of spiritual capital. To shift any culture, corporate or otherwise, we have to understand the motivations (and attendant attitudes and emotions) that drive that culture in the first place. Chapters Three and Four offer a new, systematic way to diagnose the motivational and emotional state of a present culture. This is done through offering a new scale of motivations that both mirrors and extends Abraham Maslow's well-known pyramid of needs. To use these chapters properly requires cultivation and use of emotional intelligence, particularly the component of EQ that develops emotional self-awareness.

Chapters Five through Eight introduce the new concept of spiritual intelligence, define its twelve qualities and principles of transformation, and describe how these can be used to shift individuals and their culture from a state of acting from lower motivations (fear, greed, anger, and self-assertion) to one of acting from higher motivations (exploration, cooperation, power-within, mastery, and higher service).

Chapter Nine describes how this shift actually happens and can be diagnosed in a given organizational culture. It looks in depth at the eight issues that dominate corporate culture (communication, fairness, relationships, trust, power, truth, flexibility, and empowerment) and how these are influenced by the twelve processes of SQ transformation introduced earlier. Chapter Ten discusses the leadership elite who can bring about and embody cultural shift. This introduces the crucial leadership categories of "knights" and "masters," those who make the new culture (knights) and those who embed the new culture within the practices of the organization (masters). Finally, Chapter Eleven, the concluding chapter, argues that spiritual capital is still a valid and workable form of capitalism, and summarizes what we, as individuals, can do to make it happen.

You will see some science in the book. Familiarity with a few discoveries of the most recent neuroscience is necessary to understand how spiritual intelligence is enabled by structures in the brain. In particular, it's essential to be aware of the recent discovery of the "God Spot," a mass of neural tissue in the brain's temporal lobes that enables human beings to have a sense of the sacred and a longing for the deeper things in life.

Chaos theory, too, plays a role in the book's development. Chaos (and the associated science of complexity) is one of the twentieth century's "new sciences." It describes nonlinear and self-organizing systems poised at the boundary between order and disorder, between stability and instability. Such systems include anthills, beehives, the weather, the stock market, and the human immune system. I argue that any organization or society with the capacity to be creative and sustainable in today's unstable and crisis-riven world will have the characteristics of what chaos and complexity theory calls "complex adaptive systems." These characteristics include holism, diversity, spontaneity, self-organization, emergence, and coevolution between the systems and their environments.

All living systems, ourselves included, are complex adaptive systems, and human consciousness itself displays the characteristics of complexity in many of its abilities. In Chapter Six, I discuss how and why the properties of complex adaptive systems make it possible to derive most of the qualities that distinguish spiritual intelligence.

A great many subthemes and minor threads run through the book, all necessary to put real flesh on the bones of the main theme. This is not a single-idea book, though I hope the brief road map that I have provided here will allow readers to experience the book as an integrated whole. Ultimately, spiritual capital is not just an idea but a whole new paradigm, and new paradigms contain a richness and complexity that branch out in many complementary directions.

The Monster That Consumes Itself

I n Ovid's tales from Greek mythology, we learn of a wealthy timber merchant named Erisychthon (Er-is-ya-thon). Erisychthon is a greedy man who thinks only of profit. Nothing is sacred to him. But on Erisychthon's land there is a special tree beloved of the gods. Prayers of the faithful are tied to its prodigious branches and holy spirits dance round its magnificent trunk. Erisychthon cares nothing for this. He looks at the tree and assesses the volume of timber it will produce, then he takes an axe to it. Against all protest he chops until the tree is withered and fallen and all divine life that inhabited the tree has fled. But one of the gods puts a curse on Erisychthon for his greed. From that day forward, Erisychthon is consumed by an insatiable hunger. He begins by eating all his stores, then he turns all his wealth into food he can consume. Still not satisfied, he consumes his wife and children. In the end, Erisychthon is left with nothing to consume but his own flesh. He eats himself.

Executive Voices of Business-as-Usual

"The environment is the government's responsibility."

"Never mind what our product is. Just help us sell it more effectively."

"The only purpose of this business is to meet our customers' demands and to make a profit out of it."

"We don't know what's outside the window, and we don't care."

"I don't think we have to trouble our minds with all this deep stuff to run our company effectively."

"I'm only in this job for the money."

"I don't think it's our responsibility to think about future generations. Our job is to satisfy our customers now."

"We can't afford to think beyond now. We have to protect ourselves and our profits."

Of a monster no longer a man. And so,
At last, the inevitable.
He began to savage his own limbs.
And there, at a final feast, devoured himself.[1]

Erisychthon is the ultimate symbol of purely economic man, and his fate is that of a way of living life, or of doing business, that is not sustainable. But he is a symbol held up to us by today's capitalism and business as we know it. He is a symbol that may represent the self-destructive fate not just of business but of our whole culture if we allow the narrow values of today's short-term, money-obsessed business ethic to dominate our broader lives and choices.

In this book, I want to look first at the assumptions and mind-set that underlie capitalist business as we know it. What are its basic values? Its primary motives? The things it takes for granted? What assumptions does business make about nature, human nature, and human motivation? Why are such assumptions and values unsustainable? Why do these assumptions ensnare business in an ultimately self-consuming spiral of behavior? Why is business as we know it today set ultimately to kill business?

How It Is Now

Modern capitalism as currently defined has only two *basic* assumptions about humanity. First, it assumes that human beings are primarily economic beings, with what Adam Smith called a "natural propensity to truck, barter and exchange." Second, capitalism assumes that human beings will always act so as to pursue our own rational self-interest, or at least our hunches about what will benefit ourselves. In business terms, these principles are mirrored by the pursuit of profit for its own sake and by the assumption that every business exists to maximize its own self-interest—the profits of its shareholders measured in quarterly returns.

These two basic, spoken assumptions of capitalism are underpinned by other, sometimes unconscious assumptions. Capitalism assumes that the earth is here to provide us with resources, and that these resources are unlimited. It also assumes that each agent or corporation is an island unto itself whose actions have no unwanted consequences, and whose interests are under its own self-control. There is, too, the more general assumption that the whole world of business is an island unto itself, an enterprise that can be conducted without regard to or concern for wider issues. "We don't know what's outside the window, and we don't care."

At the heart of capitalism and business-as-usual lies a very narrow definition of what it means to be human and to be engaged in human enterprise. Human beings are measured by thirst for profit and by capacity to consume. Employees are measured by their capacity to produce what others can consume. Viewed merely as consumers, customers and employees are not seen as people who value certain things, who harbor loyalties and passions, who strive and dream, who seek a particular quality of life. Big consumers (the wealthy) have more value than small consumers (the poor). Capitalism's assumption that we will always act so as to pursue our own self-interest carries the underlying assumption that human beings are essentially selfish, that we will always act to promote "number one."

Bolstered by intellectual trends like Newtonian science and its accompanying technology and by Darwinian "survival of the fittest," capitalism's own "laws of motion" (law of competition, law of profit maximization, law of capital accumulation) have locked business-as-usual into a ruthless pursuit of competitive advantage in a world whose resources its own practices are constantly diminishing. This is not sustainable. Like Erisychthon, business is destined ultimately to consume first its own resources and then itself. We see this in the repeated fate of many Fortune 500 companies, which don't sustain themselves for even five years.

Why is business-as-usual unsustainable? On the surface—and no less valid because constantly talked about—are issues like the exhaustion of resources and accompanying environmental damage. At present rates of consumption, petroleum supplies are reckoned to last for perhaps another fifty years. As the Third World develops, these rates of consumption can only increase. As I began this book, vast population areas of the country where I live (England) were under floodwater. Global warming, we are warned, is set to continue and with it the extreme weather conditions that bring devastation to previously stable population centers and to the businesses that thrived within them. Environmental pollution and the global warming to which it is leading are also melting the polar ice caps, thus leading within fifty to a hundred years to a rise in sea levels that will flood most of the world's major coastal cities. Many scientists are now warning that this could occur even within the next ten years. Before or as that happens, the melting of the ice caps is set to reverse the Gulf Stream that protects northern Europe from being a frozen wasteland. These are not problems facing some distant, unfathomable future. The children of today's business and political leaders will inherit this legacy in their lifetimes. *We* may live to see it.

There are other obvious problems for the sustainability of business (and accompanying political strategies) as currently practiced. The assumption that human beings are primarily consumers favors the big consumers over the small. This has led to increasing unevenness in the distribution of the world's wealth, not just between nations and geographical areas, but often *within* wealthy societies. Extreme wealth lives side by side with the most extreme poverty in nations such as India, the United States, and Brazil. Such imbalance bodes ill for political and social stability within societies where it exists (high crime, family breakdown, civil unrest, a sense of despair, domestic terrorism, potential revolutions).

Between rich and poor nations, inequality leads to the pressure on the poor to migrate to wealthier areas, swelling populations of illegal immigrants and the accompanying social and political unrest. It creates both a global underclass and various domestic underclasses. Extreme inequality adds to the sense that "globalization" means simply the colonization of the poor by the wealthy capitalist world. This leads to humiliation and rage. It fuels the hatred of terrorists who both envy and fear the wealthy in developed nations. All these things are bad for business. Capitalism creates a shadow of itself that, like Erisychthon's greed, reaches round to consume itself.

Less obviously, the assumption that human beings are purely economic creatures who live to make money increases the stress and exhaustion of the "winners" who serve the existing system. Other values—time with the family, time to relax, time to nourish inner needs, time to enjoy the accumulated wealth, opportunity to find fulfillment in the work we are doing, a sense of fundamental purpose in life—are sacrificed in the pursuit of ever more profit, ever bigger monetary growth. People who lead and work within the mighty corporations generating all this profit might be tempted to ask, with Charles Handy, "What is this business for and to whom does it belong? Are we who work in these businesses, be they social or commercial, their instruments or something more than that?"[2]

The major cause of stress in most of our lives today is a loss of meaning. Things change so quickly and so constantly, so many of our old certainties no longer apply, that we have lost our essential bearings. There is reengineering, downsizing, redefinition of jobs, corporate break-ups and mergers, the musical chairs of new CEOs, the often-sham offers of empowerment and autonomy, the short-term contracts and their diminution of loyalty, commitment, and trust. And that's just business stress. In our private lives we experience the erosion of moral

and religious certainties, changes in family and relationship structure, constant mobility, loss, divorce, retirement, and the death of loved ones. Twenty-first-century
life has become like the Caucus Race in Lewis Carroll's
Alice Through the Looking Glass. Someone says "Let's
play a game"—but there are no rules and no clear sense
of the playing field's boundaries Someone shouts
"Begin!" and we all start running around. Then, at some
arbitrary point, someone shouts "Stop!" There are no
winners and no losers. We haven't a clue what it's all
about. We are left with nothing from the effort but stress
and the kind of world-weariness described by the
English poet William Wordsworth,

> The world is too much with us; late and soon,
> Getting and spending, we lay waste our powers:
> Little we see in Nature that is ours;
> We have given our hearts away, a sordid boon!
>
> This Sea that bares her bosom to the moon;
> The winds that will be howling at all hours,
> And are up-gathered now like sleeping flowers;
> For this, for everything, we are out of tune;
>
> It moves us not. . . .

Meaninglessness and the stress to which it gives rise
is the major cause of illness in the developed world
today. Diseases like depression, anxiety, chronic fatigue
syndrome, alcoholism, drug abuse, and suicide are obviously stress-related. But mainstream medicine now
recognizes a crucial stress factor in the so-called physical illnesses of high blood pressure, heart disease, cancer, and even Alzheimer's disease. Stress depresses the
human immune system's ability to fight off any disease.
Stress releases a constant stream of adrenaline for "fight
or flight" behavior, along with other stress hormones

that raise concentration to a critical height—in the short term. Over an extended period, they burn us out.

Stress and exhaustion are clearly bad for the people who suffer them. They lead to disease and premature death. But stressed and exhausted people are also bad for business. They reduce overall creativity and productivity, they are prone to illness and absence from work, they cost companies and national economies money. *Stress-related illness costs the United Kingdom 3.9 billion pounds sterling annually. It costs the United States 10 percent of gross national product each year.*[3]

Again, business as we know it, business that assumes money and only money is the bottom line, is unsustainable because it has led to a leadership crisis within top companies. The problems and challenges facing business today are enormous: rapid change, globalization, new technology, greater customer expectations, political, social, and ecological crises. Yet, as professor John Hunt from the London Business School points out, devoting one's life to making ever more money for the shareholders isn't ultimately very inspiring.[4] As an executive from Shell USA said to me recently, "The trouble with corporate life is that it is *essentially* dispiriting. Corporations are about making money. They define work as the pursuit of money. But we human beings are essentially spiritual creatures. We are on a lifelong quest for meaning. So our corporate lives exclude what we really care about."

Great leaders usually want to serve great causes, want their lives and their work to count for something, want to make a difference in life. Such people are attracted to politics, medicine, research, education. They are seldom found at the top of large corporations. Many who were have left to work for nonprofit organizations like Save the Children or the major NGOs. This critical shortage of great leaders is bad for business.

As the pool of potentially great leaders has drained, leaving behind the pure money seekers, business has become increasingly dirty business. Capitalism itself has never had any moral principles or framework. It is an economic theory, not a moral or social philosophy. The market, pure and simple, is its bottom line. Very early capitalism was contained within the moral and spiritual vision of Christianity, hence all those altruistic Quaker businessmen of the Victorian era. But as ethics and values have eroded generally in society, business is left with the ethics of Gordon Gecko, the ruthless corporate raider portrayed in *Wall Street*. New millennium business has been exposed as a moral quagmire, where biggest crocodiles will use any kind of cheating, fraud, or false accounting to fill their own bellies. As John Plender said in his recent book *Going off the Rails,* "The American way of doing business has been hijacked by the values of a financial community that is so preoccupied with trading and dealmaking that it has lost sight of the purpose of its own business. There is indeed a crisis of legitimacy in modern capitalism."

Not content with cheating society at large (all those tax evasions), or even their customers, the leaders of companies like Enron, WorldCom, and a host of others were willing ruthlessly to cheat their own stockholders. In Plender's words, "Everyone in the [Enron] story was involved in potential conflicts of interest. And everyone—including the watchdogs—had been bought by Enron in one way or another." As the consequent fall in stock prices and market instability have shown, dirty business is bad for business.

Finally, business today is killing business because it is locked into a short-term, problem-solving, profit-maximizing mentality. In the words of this book, business is not using its whole brain, not using its full intelligence. If my mind is focused on the money I can make in three months' time (quarterly returns), my whole perspective is narrow and limited. I use my rational, linear, problem-solving intelligence to solve immediate problems that stand in the way of a quick buck. I am blind to broader issues like the long-term viability of the planet or even the shorter-term viability of my own society or company, or the lifestyle and values I am forcing upon myself and my family. I don't reflect. I don't plan ahead. I don't look at "the big picture." I don't allot adequate time or devote sufficient resources to the research needs of my company. I don't look at long-term safety features or future growth.

In Britain recently, we have seen our entire rail infrastructure crack. For months the trains virtually could not run. Too late, Railtrack (the private company in charge of Britain's rail network) saw not only that present lines had deteriorated beyond acceptable standards of safety but also that wholly inadequate plans had been considered for how to enable the nation's rail network to serve the pressing needs of future traffic. Why? Short-term profit and the short-term thinking it had spawned. Investors wanted good quarterly dividends; senior managers felt their job was to ensure them. As is common in large corporations, managers' bonuses were linked to quarterly results.

Railtrack's story is not unusual. Short-term, uncommitted investment by huge, anonymous investment funds is the scourge of today's business, depriving company leaders of control over their own planning and debasing the whole ethic of doing business. Such investments, and their inflationary and destabilizing effect, were at the heart of the crisis that struck the Tiger Economies in the late 1990s. Short-term, get-rich-quick investments were also responsible for the catastrophic decline in Marconi shares at the beginning of the new millennium. Money-making has become money-grubbing, and money-grubbing is bad for business.

A Still Deeper Nonsustainability

The issues I have discussed thus far are often talked about, and are no less real or threatening for that. But a far deeper underlying issue is at stake in the attitudes and practices of capitalism as we know it. This is the issue of what sustains or threatens our humanity itself, and the high civilizations that that humanity has enabled. In asking if capitalism is sustainable, we must ask whether it serves our deepest human values and aspirations. We must ask if it will enable the survival of the human species, and whether it can sustain the human enterprise in the larger context of such vital questions as, What is the meaning and purpose of human life?

In the 1960s, the psychologist Abraham Maslow gave voice and credibility to capitalism as we know it with the famous "pyramid of needs" illustrated in Figure 1.1. Maslow's pyramid created a paradigm of the human condition that gave precedence to the need for survival, physical survival at all costs. In close second was the need for security, the security of myself and mine. The sense that such needs are taken as primary for business-as-usual is reflected in some of the opening remarks I quoted, such as "We can't afford to think about future generations. We must protect ourselves and our profits."

Maslow's pyramid makes room for higher needs, the needs for social connections, for self-esteem, and for what he calls self-actualization—the need for personal meaning and spiritual and psychological growth. But in his model these higher needs can be considered only if the more basic needs for survival and security are first assured. First and foremost we are animals, "naked apes," who only later, if conditions allow, aspire to become human beings.

Frederick Herzberg's famous 1959 study of what motivates people at work gave the lie to Maslow's hierarchy so far as what causes most dissatisfaction or gives most satisfaction among employees. While "basic" factors or needs like company policy and administration, relationships with supervisors or peers, salary, work conditions, and security gave rise to *dissatisfaction* if they were not adequate, but they gave rise to *no satisfaction* if they were adequate. The more positive quality of finding

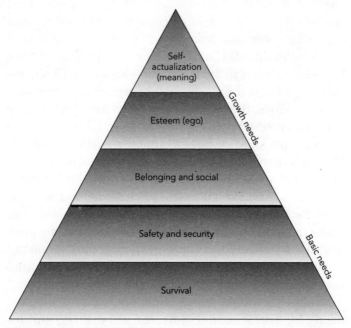

Figure 1.1 *Maslow's Hierarchy of Needs*

satisfaction in one's work and thus feeling highly motivated depended on factors like growth, advancement, responsibility, the work itself, recognition, and a sense of achievement.[5] These are things Maslow regarded as "higher needs."

It is a basic argument of this book and of all that follows that in a developed culture like ours Maslow's pyramid of needs is upside down. (See Figure 1.2.) Most of us in the wealthy Western world have our basic needs for food and security met as a birthright. Those who have experienced fulfillment of both higher and lower needs regard the higher ones as more important. They bring more happiness and satisfaction. Since Maslow's work was done nearly half a century ago, anthropologists, neuroscientists, and psychologists have reached a

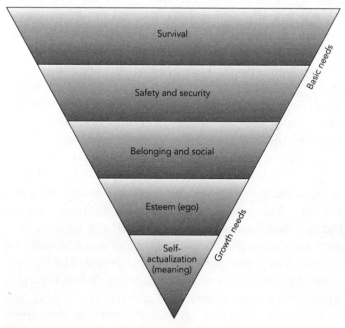

Figure 1.2 *Inverting Maslow's Hierarchy*

far deeper understanding of human nature and the origins of our humanity. We know today that human beings are by definition primarily creatures of meaning and value (that is, of "self-actualization"). We need a sense of meaning and driving purpose in our lives. Without it we become ill or we die.

Indeed, it was a primitive quest for meaning, to know and explore what was beyond the horizon, that first brought our species down from the trees some four million years ago. It was a pressure to communicate symbols and meanings between individuals and within early human groups that gave rise to language, and to the coevolution of the large human forebrain that language skills require.[6] Later the human brain grew masses of neural tissue in the temporal lobe areas that gave expression to still deeper needs for meaning—a need to ask why we are here, how we fit into the larger scheme of things, how we came to be born and why we must die, how we relate to the "gods," and similar weighty questions. This area of the brain has been named "the God Spot," and will be discussed at greater length in a later chapter. The God Spot accounts for the presence of religious ideas, rites, and rituals since the founding of the earliest known human societies.

Scientists have also discovered in this past half-century the role that altruism has played in the development of human societies. We have not always been out for "number one," and indeed we would not be here today if selfishness had always ruled the day. Survival itself depends upon the willingness of some to sacrifice themselves for others or for the group. Self-esteem depends upon knowing that one has "done the right thing" by life and others, and survival (the will to live and the ability to live with oneself) becomes impossible without it.

The psychologist Viktor Frankl (*Man's Search for Meaning*) noted that concentration camp inmates in Nazi Germany who betrayed others for the sake of their own survival could not live with themselves afterward.[7] The suicide of the great twentieth-century writer Primo Levi was believed to follow from his inability to live with what he had done to survive Auschwitz. By contrast, countless stories exist of people who have willingly sacrificed their lives (survival) for the sake of others or for the sake of causes in which they believe. In Frankl's study, those Auschwitz inmates who had strong religious beliefs or strong political ideals survived better than those without. The Muslim suicide bombers who attacked the World Trade Center and the Pentagon on September 11 made such a sacrifice, as have countless others in the Middle East. We may detest what they do, but we cannot deny they were willing to die for what *they* saw as a higher cause—however evil and distorted this cause may be.

In earlier hunter-gatherer societies, it required a group to hunt successfully; an individual alone could not survive. Thus the need for "unselfish" genes—which still survive today. (We were all hunters only ten thousand years ago.) The same need for group cooperation existed in farming communities and family-based enterprises only two centuries ago. We have evolved to be group animals as well as individuals and are often alienated by today's essentially selfish and individualist Western culture. Even recent studies of what drives a healthy market have shown that a combination of selfishness and altruism (competition and cooperation, egocentricity and reciprocity) ensures the optimum market trading conditions.[8]

It is reported that at the end of his life, Abraham Maslow himself came to feel that his pyramid of needs was upside down. The deep crisis of meaning—lack of belief in anything, low standards of morality, ruthless selfishness and consequent low self-esteem, absence of purpose and value, sense of boredom—that characterized much of twentieth-century life in the developed Western world is testament to capitalism's priorities being upside down. The selfishness and materialism that result from capitalist assumptions and values have raised perhaps for the first time in known human history the possibility that our humanity itself may not be sustainable. If we lose touch with or seriously damage the core of our humanity—our higher aspirations, values, and potentialities—then we really do become no more than the naked ape. I strongly suspect that might be very bad for business itself.

Another Way?

Most people who consider the costs and nonsustainability of capitalism and business as we know it would say, "There has to be another way!" Given a broader and more realistic understanding of human nature and human motivation, business-as-usual cannot be seen as a fully human enterprise. Its narrow and wrong-headed assumptions that human beings are essentially economic creatures, and selfish ones at that, do not accord with the facts as we know them today. Nor to they speak to the hunger our culture feels to rise above the materialist quagmire in which we have become stuck.

Taking for granted that it is global business that has the money and the power to make a significant difference in today's troubled world, this book envisages business raising its sights above the financial bottom line. It envisages business becoming a vocation, like the higher professions. This entails business becoming more ser-vice and value oriented, largely eliminating the assumed natural distinction between private enterprise and pub-lic institutions. It envisages business taking responsibil-ity for the world in which it operates and from which it creates its wealth. And it envisages a higher proportion of business leaders becoming "servant leaders"—leaders who serve not just stockholders, colleagues, employees, products, and customers, but leaders who serve the community, the planet, humanity, the future, life itself. Leaders who dare to "look outside the window."

But getting from business-as-usual to business-as-it-could-be is no simple matter. A little talk about corporate social responsibility, some discussion of "vision and val-ues," and giving employees little plastic "values" cards to carry around in their wallets are not going to change very much. What is required is a whole new business paradigm, a paradigm shift that embraces our basic concepts of wealth and capital themselves and that brings on board a new, living understanding of what a business system *is,* and how such systems can be man-aged intelligently. These in turn require that we look in some depth at the nature of both business systems and human intelligence.

In the pages that follow, I will try to broaden the understanding of capital to include the new concepts of "social capital" and "spiritual capital." When you look more fully at what it means to be human and thus what it would mean for business to serve that humanity, it becomes possible to contrast holistic, dynamic, self-organizing, and creative complex adaptive systems with the mechanistic systems that inspired original capital-ism. That will lead to ways to turn a modern business into a fully human, complex adaptive system that is not just sustainable but "deeply sustainable."

Throughout, I will discuss the origins, nature and organizing power of the intelligence needed to build these systems—"spiritual intelligence," or SQ (wisdom), contrasting it with the more familiar IQ of traditional capitalism and the more recent emphasis on EQ (emotional intelligence) of some modern systems thinkers. The book will use this understanding of systems and intelligence to offer a new business model and a new basis for strategic planning that are compatible with the wider purpose of business-as-it-could-be and with the amassing of spiritual capital.

What Is Spiritual Capital?

"Spiritual capital" is a new paradigm. It requires that we radically change our mind-set about the philosophical foundations and the practice of business. It is not anticapitalist—or even noncapitalist, but it does require the addition of moral and social dimensions to capitalism. Spiritual capital itself is not monetary wealth, but it argues the possibility of making a profit—perhaps even more profit—by doing business in a wider context of meaning and value. It can generate profit that both draws on and adds to the wealth of the human spirit and to general human well-being.

In Chapter One, I described the shadow side of capitalism—and most of my points were not new. These same observations and criticisms have been made by socialists, communists, environmentalists, and some sociologists. But the alternative visions they have offered have not worked either. Marxism offers a clearcut example.

According to Marx, capitalism appeals to humanity's selfish motives and leads to the exploitation of the weak by the powerful. This in turn breeds suffering and resentment. Marx believed that the whole problem lay in the class structure that supported capitalism. If we could rid ourselves of this class structure, mankind's highest motives would be unleashed. Our innate community spirit would prevail and we would have "the Brotherhood of Man." Economically, *The Communist Manifesto* maintained, wealth would be divided happily according to the principle, "From each according to his abilities; to each according to his needs."

We know that Communism did not work in any of the societies where it was tried. Socialism, too, has failed to compete with the economic successes of capitalism. I think that the real failing of Marx's thought was twofold. First, he did not understand that, capitalism or no capitalism, most people often act from selfish motivation. We are not the pure altruists that Marx assumed. In all Communist countries, armies of bureaucrats, overseers, and enforcement agencies had to be used, and these in turn could be bribed. Corruption and enslavement were rife.

Marx's second failing was his inability to understand the true nature of higher motivation and therefore of the forces needed to shift human motivation from lower to higher. Marx, like the capitalists, reduced everything to material needs. He replaced the philosopher Hegel's "Spirit" with money, entirely missing the reality that the path toward acting from higher motivations rests on a deeply spiritual foundation.

Dissatisfaction with capitalism, and the failure of communism, have moved some thinkers to suggest a "third way." This is essentially the inspiration for the brand of European social democracy promoted by Anthony Giddens and Tony Blair. Unfortunately, this has not fired the hearts or changed the motivations of many people. It lacks firm philosophical, economic, and psychological basis. On the whole it tends to be a well-meant grab bag of various free-market and central planning ideas. Where the private sector has been brought in to work with the public sector (as in health care), the capitalist ethos has tended to control and distort the aims of public sector service. No *real* "third way" has been articulated that draws its force from the deeper realm of human motivation and how to shift it. "Spiritual capital" is an attempt to outline that new paradigm.

It is often best to illustrate a new paradigm by example. Not all companies today are stuck in the Erisychthon scenario, and those few who have pioneered a new way can make the task of following suit seem less daunting. To lay the foundations for seeing how the ideas of capital, wealth, and the role of business in society can be expanded, here is a look at one company that has amassed something more than material profit.

Merck Pharmaceutical was founded by a man with a vision. He wanted "to bring medicine to the patient who needs it." Along the way he and his successors have made a great deal of money, but that is not all they have done.

Merck's Story

In 1995, Merck and Co. was America's largest pharmaceutical company.[1] It had an annual turnover of $16.7 billion, with net profits running at $3.3 billion. Throughout most of the 1990s, Merck had been voted the "most admired" company by *Fortune* magazine, and *Business Week* ran a cover story calling it "The Miracle Company," lauding both its research and management practices. Especially noted for its innovation in the lab, and with a mid-1990s R&D budget of $1.5 billion, Merck had invented such revolutionary drugs as the cholesterol-lowering Mevacor, the antihypertensive drug Vasotec, new asthma therapies, and the world's first-ever chicken pox vaccine—all part of a highly profitable company success story that has brought improved health care to much of the world.

Like most large drug companies, Merck had on the whole focused on developing products that would ensure large profits—that is, products for the wealthy, developed world. But then an opportunity arose that fell outside that usual business model. The opportunity, which brought an unforeseen chance to cure one of the Third World's most insidious and disabling infections, meant that the company had to rethink some of capitalism's most sacred priorities.

In Africa, the Middle East, and throughout much of South America, some 340,000 people are blind as the result of being bitten by a blackfly carrying a parasite that destroys sight. Another million suffer partial blindness from the same cause, while 18 million are infected with the parasite and 85 million at risk of being so. The parasite causes onchocerciasis, or "oncho," known popularly as "river blindness."

In the late '70s, while developing a hugely effective and vastly profitable veterinary drug that kills a similar parasite in domestic livestock, Merck scientists found they had discovered a closely related compound that could prevent river blindness. Further, the compound, named "Mectizan," need only be administered as one tablet swallowed once a year. Merck was earning its nickname as "the miracle company" yet again. The problem? Whereas its veterinary equivalent was earning the company over $1 billion in annual sales by the end of its first decade, Mectizan's potential market was to people and governments in The Third World who had no money to pay for it. No world body was willing to finance Mectizan's development and the necessary safety tests, never mind its distribution to the people who needed it, most of whom lived in dreadfully isolated areas.

Despite the lack of any profit prospects, indeed despite the knowledge that it would have to fund all development and clinical trials itself, Merck decided to go ahead with Mectizan production. When no customers could be found at any price, the company took the wholly unorthodox decision simply to give the drug away to anyone who needed it—a gift worth about $250 million. The result? By the mid-1990s, with the help of WHO, The World Bank, various Third World governments and NGOs, Mectizan was on target for reaching 15 million people in sixteen participating countries.

In the Mectizan saga, Merck's material gain was nil. But the good will earned, and the sense of achievement gained—and the consequent high morale of the company's scientists—were worth it. Besides, in past such episodes in Japan, when after World War II Merck had distributed streptomycin (at no profit) to solve the country's enormous TB scourge, and later in China, where Merck donated its whole technology for making the hepatitis B vaccine to prevent liver cancer, such good will eventually paid off in huge dividends earned by other Merck products. Setting one's sights on something beyond material profit can actually increase material profit in the long term.

I call the kind of capital earned by Merck in the river blindness episode "spiritual capital." It is capital earned from serving deep meaning, from serving a deep sense of purpose and from serving fundamental human values. It is a kind of capital initially measured not in dollars and cents but rather in the sense of achievement, the high morale, the gratitude, and the general increase in well-being that accompany raising the quality of human life. It is the same kind of capital earned historically by the great Quaker businesses like Clarke's Shoes and Rowntree's Chocolates, who used large proportions of their profits to ensure safer working conditions for their employees and to build schools and hospitals for the community. It is the same kind of capital earned by Islamic bankers who refuse to charge interest for money loaned but who instead share the risk with their borrowers by taking a percentage of ownership in the goods bought or enterprises built. And it is the same kind of capital earned by Coca-Cola when it offers the Indian government free use of its delivery trucks to distribute polio vaccine to the poor in isolated regions of that country, or when its "Project Peace" builds health clinics throughout rural China and Southeast Asia. See sidebar, "A Few Examples of Companies That Accrue Spiritual Capital."

Expanding Our Notion of Capital

If challenged about capitalism's prime motive of profit maximization, most businesspeople look dumbfounded and say, "Of course! It has always been that way. That is business. The whole point of business is to make a profit." But in fact the business-as-usual that we know today is only two hundred years old—out of a human history of commerce that covers at least the past forty thousand years. Today's capitalism was conceived by a small handful of British Enlightenment philosophers inspired by Newtonian physics. It was the work of thinkers like

A Few Examples of Companies That Accrue Spiritual Capital

- Amul markets the output of the 10,000 milk cooperatives in the Indian state of Gujarat. A peasant with only one bucket of milk to sell per day can earn his vital 20 rupees, competing in his own right—and regardless of caste—with larger dairy farmers. An embodiment of Mahatma Gandhi's social and economic principles, Amul has sales of $516 million annually.

- Van City, Vancouver's largest credit union, channels lending funds to customers and causes marginalized by mainstream banks—inner-city development, risky small business ventures, environmental protection projects, disadvantaged women, and investment funds for the developing world. Van City prospers with its commitment to corporate social responsibility, with $6.4 billion annual turnover and $39 million annual profit.

- Coca-Cola has put its distribution network in India at the service of the Indian national government to distribute polio vaccine to remote rural areas. It has a similar project in Africa to distribute AIDS medication. No extra cost, enormous gain in spiritual capital. Its "Project Peace" is building health clinics throughout rural China and Southeast Asia.

- British Petroleum has adopted (and takes very seriously!) the new motto, "Beyond Petroleum." This makes BP an energy company instead of an oil company. It has a heavy investment in developing hydrogen and other alternative energy technologies that both reduce dependence on scarce and damaging hydrocarbon fuels and provide energy for the postpetroleum future. It is keeping profits high *by way of* reducing environmental damage.

- Starbucks, the global coffee shop chain, sees social responsibility to coffee growers, their communities, and environments as an integral part of company vision and its implementation. Paying 240 percent

> above base world price to its coffee growers for
> beans, the company also invests in health clinics,
> schools, credit unions, and bio-diversity schemes in
> growers' communities.

Adam Smith and John Stuart Mill, men who admired
Newton's work and who in their turn contributed to
Frederick Taylor's paradigm of scientific management
theory. They saw the individual business as part of a vast
economic machine oiled by money. Their idea of capital
was solely that of *material capital,* capital that can be
measured in money.

But *capital* has a wider meaning. In the *Oxford English
Dictionary,* capital is defined as "that which confers
wealth, profit, advantage or power." Capitalism, the economic doctrine that underpins business-as-usual, gives
the narrowest possible definition to all these terms.
Wealth is taken to equal money, so that the wealth that
makes the world go round is material wealth, and profit
is material profit. Advantage is something that confers
material advantage, an advantage measured in money or
in the power to manipulate people or the environment to
maximize its holder's (usually money-based) interests.

That view leads straight into the Erisychthon scenario, where business consumes itself and all that we
value about our humanity along with it. To escape, we
need to expand our whole concept of wealth. We need a
concept of wealth that enriches rather than impover-
ishes the human spirit, a notion of wealth that inspires
people to give of their best in creating it. To avoid the
shadow, or dark, side of capitalism, we need a notion of
wealth that accrues from a responsible and compassionate inclusion of the have-nots, and from a committed
resolve to meet basic human needs. Ignoring this has

led to the violent reaction we see against capitalism on the streets of Seattle and Davos, and to the hatred that fuels anticapitalist and anti-Western terrorism. For those who work in business, we also need a notion of wealth that reflects meaningful and fulfilling personal and working lives.

Some recent attempts have been made to expand the notion of capital. We hear a lot in company circles today about "intellectual capital" and "human capital," but these just extend the idea of material worth to ideas and people. They attempt to put a price tag on employees' creativity and skills. They add nothing new to the concept of capital itself.

In the past few years, some economists and sociologists have brought new thinking to the field by writing about "social capital." By social capital, they mean both the material wealth and the social benefit gained by a society that has low crime, low divorce and illegitimacy rates, low litigation figures, high literacy, and a high degree of trust. This was the subject of Francis Fukuyama's recent book, *Trust.* Asian societies are said to be high in social capital because of their basic social stability, Western ones low in it. As opposed to mere material worth, social capital also measures the raised quality of life in a society.

In the corporate world, social capital has come to mean specifically the wealth accrued by the quality of the relationships in an organization—how well people communicate, how much they trust each other and their senior executives, how they function as teams, whether the emotional intelligence of the group is high, whether there are effective networks of acquaintance and cooperation, and the like. The stress is on *interpersonal* relations within the company. The social capital built up by such qualities and relationships is said to be in the common ownership of the group and to need regular maintenance. It is a feature of the organization's *internal culture*. Significant social capital is also seen as a feature of the organization that underpins greater material wealth.[2] Companies that score high on the quality of internal relationships tend to make more profit.

Hewlett-Packard, for instance, is famous for its high level of social capital—the very high degree of commitment, pride, and trust shared by its employees. The HP Way ensures effective communication of the company's basic vision throughout every level, teams function effectively, and the "single status" policy of the company ensures that everyone feels appreciated and adequately rewarded. As Lynda Gratton from London Business School comments, "Commitment, pride and trust are critical to sustaining ongoing change at HP and senior executives believe these are major factors in the ability of the business to remain flexible and to increase turnover and profitability at a rate of 20% per annum, year on year, without significantly increasing employee numbers."[3] In the downturn that hit the American economy at the beginning of the new millennium, Hewlett-Packard was one of the very few companies to maintain a high rate of growth.

As narrowly interpreted in corporate circles, the high social capital of a given company may well benefit employees, customers, and shareholders, though it ignores the broader dimension of lending stability to wider society. I think this wider dimension cannot be addressed by business without the foundation of a deeper spiritual vision. We need to have some sense of what human life and the human enterprise are *about,* and how to improve them.

"Spiritual capital," the subject of this book, takes the broadening of capital—and its associated wealth, advantage, profit, and power—a stage further. Indeed I believe it transcends the usual notion of capital altogether. Defining a sense of wider meaning, the possession of an enlivening or inspiring vision, the implementation of fundamental human values, and a deep sense of wider purpose as the "commodities of exchange," those organizations or individuals that act from such a wider context and broader concerns are said to be invested with spiritual capital. Our spiritual capital is our shared meaning, our shared purpose, our shared vision of what most deeply matters in life—and how these are implemented in our lives and in our behavioral strategies. It is capital that is increased by drawing on the resources of the human spirit.

In a tidy phrase, *spiritual capital is the amount of spiritual knowledge and expertise available to an individual or a culture,* where *spiritual* is taken to mean "meaning, values, and fundamental purposes."

Both social capital and spiritual capital bear on the growing sense of a need for wider corporate social responsibility—the realization that business is a *part of* the wider community and must accept some real responsibility *for* it. But spiritual capital takes this notion, too, still further. Spiritual capital, as I define it, is wealth that helps to make the future of humanity sustainable as well as wealth that nourishes and sustains the human spirit. It is reflected in what a community or an organization

Spiritual capital is reflected in what a community or organization

- *Exists for*
- *Aspires to*
- *Takes responsibility for*

believes in, what a community or an organization *exists for,* what it *aspires to,* what it *takes responsibility for.* It is only when these aspects of spirit are nourished and seen to be served that we can go on to build the social and material wealth that sustain daily life.

It is my conviction that spiritual capital is the bedrock of an organization or a society. By nurturing and sustaining the core purpose of our whole human enterprise, spiritual capital is the glue that binds us together. It provides us with a moral and a motivational framework, an ethos, a *spirit.* It sustains, underpins, and enriches both material capital and social capital. But we shall also see in the work that follows that spiritual capital can be a dynamic factor within an organization. Organizations rich in spiritual capital are not just sustainable, they are evolutionary. By going through the process of raising its spiritual capital, an organization transforms itself from the inside. It moves. It has life. It has a deep sense of purpose and direction. In the words of complexity science, it becomes "a complex, adaptive, self-organizing system." All these improve the inner vitality of the organization and also its ability to function effectively in and contribute to its wider environment. This follows from what I mean by *spiritual* in the first place.

What I Mean by Spiritual

When I speak of "spiritual capital," or later of the "spiritual intelligence" needed to build such capital, I do not mean anything to do with religion or with theological belief systems. I am not suggesting that companies become more spiritual in the sense of building shrines in the reception foyer or calling their employees to

> The spiritual in human beings makes us ask *why* we are doing what we are doing and makes us seek some fundamentally better way of doing it. It makes us want our lives and enterprises to make a difference.

prayer. The word *spiritual* comes originally from the Latin *spiritus,* which means "that which gives life or vitality to a system." This is spirituality seen as an enhancement of life in the world, rather than as a monkish emphasis on other-worldly values. For human beings, that which gives life—indeed that which gives unique definition—to our humanity is our need to place our enterprises in a frame of wider meaning and purpose. The spiritual in human beings makes us ask *why* we are doing what we are doing and makes us seek some fundamentally *better way* of doing it. It makes us want our lives and enterprises to *make a difference.*

- Companies concerned with amassing spiritual capital are constantly placing their goals and strategies in a wider context of meaning and value. They are constantly reframing their aims and recontextualizing the effects.
- Companies rich in spiritual capital are self-aware companies. They know what they believe in, what and whom they affect, and what they want to achieve.
- Companies that build spiritual capital are vision and value led. Their core vision is visible and inspires everything that is done. It is a deep vision. The values of spiritual capital are deep human values—saving life, raising the quality of life, improving health, education, communication,

meeting basic human needs, sustaining the global ecology, and reinforcing a sense of excellence, pride in service, and the like.

- Companies that build spiritual capital have a high sense of *holism* or connectivity. They see that business is part of the wider human enterprise, part of the wider global scenario. They feel a part of and responsible to the community, the planet, life itself. Spiritual capital takes into account that everything we do or represent in company culture (rational decisions, emotional and psychological issues, neglecting the needs of the Third World or the fears and resentments of Islam) winds up in the bottom line.

- Companies that build spiritual capital are compassionate companies. They have a sense of fellow-feeling, fellow-being with all those whom they affect or could affect. If they see need or suffering within their sphere of influence, they care and take responsibility for doing something about it.

- Companies that build spiritual capital celebrate diversity. They recognize that every point of view is necessary and that every point of view carries some validity. They recognize that wealth generated from many sources and bred from within many traditions creates a more vibrant business climate.

- Companies that build spiritual capital are field-independent. They dare to be different, dare to stand out from the crowd, dare even to be unpopular at times if necessary. This is part of their leadership role. Rather than following the trend, they set new trends. They get a sense of value and a sense of self-esteem not from how others see them but from a conviction that they are being true to their own values and vision.

- Companies that build spiritual capital raise fundamental *Why* questions. They never allow themselves to become obsessed with achieving specific goals but rather reflect on why they have chosen their goals, whether they might have chosen others, and what the full consequences of their choices are.

- Companies that build spiritual capital are always ready to be spontaneous. They don't get locked into paradigms, assumptions, or set agendas. They are not afraid of loyal dissent from within. They seek constantly to surface, and if necessary to undermine, their own assumptions. They seek to become aware of the paradigm from which their values, goals, action plans, and decisions are originating, and are willing to change that paradigm if necessary. They respond to rather than react against the environment.

- Companies that build spiritual capital seek a positive response to adversity. Business downturns, market fluctuations, changes in customer demand, and recognition of internal mistakes or miscalculations are all seen as opportunities to be creative. Large-scale global events like the terrorist attacks of September 11, 2001, massive floods, outbreaks of disease, crises in the community or in a political theater are all opportunities to reassess priorities and values, to set new goals and to renew deep purposes.

- Companies rich in spiritual capital maintain a sense of deep humility. They never take themselves too seriously, never rest on past achievements, never feel smug or self-righteous.

Spiritual capital accrues from doing the right thing, so it doesn't seek praise or unjust reward.

- Companies high in spiritual capital have a *sense of vocation.* They feel called upon to share their wealth in meeting the wider needs of community, humanity, and life itself. They are grateful for any contribution they can make to their own or the world's wealth and to the well-being of the world's people. They take nothing for granted.

I believe that companies that possess these qualities—companies high in spiritual capital—are also companies that enjoy a high competitive advantage in the marketplace. They are also companies that practice spiritual intelligence. The qualities just listed as building spiritual capital are the same qualities discussed in Chapter Five as being definitive of spiritual intelligence itself. They are the qualities that any individual, community, culture, or organization can translate into spiritual capital.

The Bottom Line: Why It's Good to Be Good

That added competitive advantage of the high-spiritual-capital enterprise is an important part of this book's whole point. It is after all the business of business to generate wealth by making profit. Business *is* society's wealth-creating mechanism. So any argument for building spiritual capital through business will have to be linked to proof that doing good can increase profit. I believe the evidence is already adequate, that those organizations and communities that act from a deeper sense of meaning, a richer vision, a deeper sense of responsibility, and a set of shared fundamental values are more likely to enjoy a longer-term competitive advantage than those that focus on their own obvious self-interest. Actions that are good for society, humanity, the planet, or any other outside entity can also result in increased material wealth for the participating individuals and organizations, and in increased worldly power in a society that has broadened its own criteria for wealth and power.

At Hewlett-Packard, for instance, it is accepted without question that it is the clearly stated and perceived and widely shared *vision* of the company that leads to HP's success at every level. At Merck Pharmaceutical, the founder's vision that "this company exists to bring medicine to the patient who needs it" drives the whole impressive R&D enterprise, as well as building the company's social capital (employee morale, team strength, shared pride, and so on).

At Starbucks, executives reckon that the company's record of solid corporate social responsibility (those high bean prices, the schools, clinics, and the rest) are an important reason why employees stay longer with the company. Every 1 percent increase in employee tenure adds $100,000 to the Starbucks annual bottom line. At the United Kingdom's Co-operative Bank, it is reckoned that ethical investment policies have brought a fivefold increase in customer deposits over the past decade and accounted for 15–18 percent of annual pretax profits.

In *Built to Last,* James Collins and Jerry Porras call companies like Hewlett-Packard, Merck, Starbucks, and the Co-operative Bank "visionary companies." In a powerful contrast, they describe the investment potential of $1 put into an ordinary stock fund and a visionary company over a period of sixty-four years (1926–1990). In that period, the \$1 invested in the ordinary fund grew to \$955, while that same \$1 invested in a visionary company grew to \$6,356. An increase of 665 percent.[4] In the words of Starbucks' director of corporate social responsibility, "Doing well and doing good are not opposites, they're companions." As I put it in this book, *it is good to be good!*

Three Levels of Corporate Social Responsibility (CSR)

In the corporate social responsibility (CSR) debate, it is now quite generally recognized that ethical policies attract customers and that nonethical policies that cause public relations disasters drive customers away. Shell learned the latter with its Brent-Spar oil platform fiasco; Nike learned it with disastrous bottom-line consequences when campaigners began to target the company's pay and working conditions in developing countries. But do all CSR programs help to build spiritual capital? I think not.

I believe it is necessary to distinguish three different levels at which companies may buy into a CSR policy. The most trivial level is CSR as mere "spin"—something that looks good for public relations purposes. The "cause-related marketing" scheme that Saatchi and Saatchi conceived for Benetton for instance, where pictures of prisoners on death row were used to advertise Benetton clothes, was on this level. The fight against capital punishment has nothing whatever to do with Benetton corporate policy or Benetton products. The campaign was intended merely to make the public associate Benetton with an emotionally charged "good cause." I don't think there is any spiritual capital to be gained from this. And indeed, such PR spin is likely to deepen customer cynicism about corporate do-gooding.

The second, somewhat deeper level, of buying into CSR is as a defensive strategy. Corporate activities that lead to PR disasters can drive away customers, shareholders, and employees. Nike's response to criticism over working conditions and child labor in its Asian sweatshops was on this level. Bad working conditions were leading to a poor bottom line, and the company was forced to address this. Their consequent do-gooding was *reactive* do-gooding. It did not spring from any deep inner vision. In a recent PriceWaterhouseCoopers study of CSR policy, it was reckoned the vast majority of firms that buy into CSR do so to avoid the negative consequences of bad publicity. Working conditions and environmental policies do often get improved by these defensive reactions, as in many Nike factories, but the motivation is not one that builds spiritual capital. It is a more childish, a more expedient, a more calculated "I'll protect myself by helping you" strategy. Again, such defensive do-gooding can backfire by deepening consumer cynicism.

The third and deepest level of CSR issues from a genuine wish to do some good that lies at the heart of a company's basic vision. Merck's wish to bring medicine to the people who need it, Starbucks' commitment to paying coffee growers a decent price for their beans and to building health and educational infrastructures in growers' communities, Hewlett-Packard's wish to provide the community with excellent, reliable, and affordable communications systems combined with contributions to community projects, many of Nokia's values-related company and community policies, Coca-Cola's widely based program to build health clinics throughout rural China, all these are at this deepest level of CSR. Companies that buy in at this level have it as part of their basic vision that one good reason for creating wealth in the first place is the good that that wealth can do. This level does build sound spiritual capital.

The Wealth We Build by Building Ourselves

Earlier, I described spiritual capital as wealth that serves "deep sustainability," wealth that builds and sustains and takes forward the core purpose of our whole human enterprise. Broader than social capital, spiritual capital makes us reconsider the very meaning of human life and raises the question of how we ourselves can build broader and richer lives for ourselves. Lives that are richer in meaning and purpose, lives that leave us with a sense of fulfillment because they are lives that have made a difference. If we are businesspeople, we do this by building our business lives. But whether in public or in private, we build spiritual capital by building ourselves.

So what does it mean or require to "build ourselves"? It means to grow as human beings, to engage in reflection and activities that put us in touch with the deeper core of our humanity. It means to find some space to get out of the noise and rush of daily life to feel for at least a few moments each day the reality of our inner lives. Building ourselves means doing things that enrich our self-awareness, our qualities of compassion, service, humility, and gratitude. It means exposing ourselves to some of that "deep stuff" that the cynical executive quoted at the beginning of this book said we don't need to run our companies.

Building ourselves, as is so often been said by spiritual leaders throughout the ages, is also more a matter of being than of doing—a process of building a *way of being*. We can't build a way of being simply by learning a new technique, reading a quick book of "10 Easy Steps to Higher Consciousness," or by attending a weekend workshop. And we certainly can't build a new way of being by cynical maneuvers aimed at impressing other people. Such behavior is usually seen through very quickly. To become better, deeper, more spiritually intelligent people, we have to grow a dimension of our being that is sensitive to the deepest meanings of human life—a sensitivity, if you like, to Plato's famous triad of values: Goodness, Truth, and Beauty. We must live our lives as a vocation, as a calling to the service of those deepest values. To do that, we must act from the higher motivations that can drive human behavior. This is a long-term project, requiring tenacity and commitment. Looking at the full range of human motivation and presenting ways to learn to act from higher motivation forms a large body of this book. Raising our motivations in life is critical to bringing about the cultural shift that many of us desire.

I will turn now to a discussion of human motivation and to the range of motivations available to us. Later chapters will indicate how we can use higher motivations to shift both our being and our behavior.

The Motivations
That Drive Us

The first two chapters have painted two very different pictures of the world. In the first, the Erisychthon scenario describes capitalism and business as we know them today: an amoral culture of short-term self-interest, profit maximization, emphasis on shareholder value, isolationist thinking, and profligate disregard of long-term consequences. I have argued that it is unsustainable. The second scenario is that of spiritual capital: a values-based culture in which wealth is accumulated to generate a decent profit while acting to raise the common good. It combines the political values of both right and left. Its emphasis is more on what Tony Blair has called "stakeholder value." But I would include as stakeholders the whole human race, present and future, the vitality of our shared culture, and the well-being of the planet itself. Spiritual capital nourishes and sustains the human spirit and is the necessary future if we are to have a future at all. The crucial question is how we can move from one scenario to the other.

* * *

Any great shift of consciousness or culture requires first that we understand both the negative consequences of staying where we are and the motivations that have put us there. Why are we here in this predicament now? Just exactly where are we starting from? And then we need to envision the future. What shift are we trying to make? What are its attractive features? And what motivations would we need to get there? This need to understand motivations and how to shift them is critical to outgrowing the crises of today's capitalism.

I believe that four primary motivations drive capitalism and business as we know them today. These are the motivations that form the culture inside which so many millions work. They are *self-assertion* (competitiveness), *anger, craving* (greed), and *fear.* The culture is highly competitive, often dog-eat-dog, and competitive people reap most of the rewards. Anger builds because people feel a sense of injustice, a lack of fairness and representation, a resentment that they are just pawns in a larger game. The greed needs no explanation. It is the primary driving force of big business today. The fear comes from a fear of making mistakes, a fear of being told off, a fear of getting fired. This is the heavy baggage, along with its accompanying attitudes, behavior, and emotional driving forces, that we have to shift.

Such motivations are all negative. They are all associated with what Abraham Maslow described as "deficiency needs," needs shared with the lower animals that don't in themselves take us to the level of being fully human. These will never take us to the higher level of spiritual capital.

I have outlined at least some of the negative consequences that follow from the motives and narrow values of business-as-usual. These include the depletion of resources, ignoring and thereby imperiling future generations, a sense of meaninglessness, and the great stress to which that leads. Many of these consequences contribute to a leadership crisis in this culture, with the "brightest and the best" migrating toward the more idealistic professions. We live in a culture riddled with corrupt self-interest, fueling both distrust and terrorism. The prominent position of such an amoral business culture driven by self-interest and greed lowers the moral standards of society at large.

At the same time, acting from higher motivations makes us happier and more stress-free. It was Maslow himself who originally suggested that for those people who have achieved basic shelter and livelihood, acting from a wish to increase self-esteem or self-actualization (positive motives) carries much more meaning and contentment than acting from lower motivations like self-preservation, self-assertion, or a desire for more money (negative motives). I quoted a more recent motivational study along these lines in Chapter One. According to American psychiatrist David Hawkins, acting from higher motivations also greatly increases our personal power.

It is easy to envision some of the positive consequences we might expect from a business culture inspired by spiritual capital. This culture would steward and renew vital resources, and it would include future generations as stakeholders. Its broader vision and deeper values would inspire participants, replacing much of today's stress with a sense of fulfillment and making leadership within it a higher vocation. Corrupted self-interest would be replaced with dedication, and its deep compassion (active compassion) would address the inequality and anger that fuel both terrorism and social unrest. A values-based business culture such as this could raise the moral standards and vision of politicians and society at large, as well as bringing more

TABLE 3.1 Two Scenarios

Scenario 1 Business-as-Usual	Scenario 2 Spiritual Capital
Depletes resources	Preserves and renews resources
Ignores future generations	Sees future generations as stakeholders
Personally dispiriting	Inspiring
Egotistic leadership	Leadership as a vocation
Stress	Sense of fulfillment
Corrupted self-interest	Dedication
Fuels terrorism and unrest	Addresses inequality and anger
Fear	Hope

happiness and a more significant sense of meaning to the many individuals concerned.

The higher motivations needed by a critical mass of the business community to ensure these more positive consequences are *mastery, creativity,* and *higher service.* But to show the implications of this, to put it in context, and to suggest ways to activate such motivations, I need to present a broader picture of the full range of human motivations and of how we can shift from lower motivations to higher ones.

The study of human motivations is as old as our ability to reflect on one another's behavior. It is a primary quality of our intelligence (IQ as well as emotional and spiritual intelligence) to ask why?—and motivations are what we describe when trying to explain our own or one another's behavior. In the Bible we read that Cain killed Abel because he was motivated by jealousy and envy. The "seven deadly sins"—lust, pride, gluttony, and the rest—are in fact seven negative motivations that drive our behavior. The Ten Commandments were an early attempt to shift that culture. Freud thought, pessimistically, that all human behavior is driven by the two primary motives of sex and aggression. Various therapists since have tried to counterbalance this by stressing motives such as love, altruism, and service.

Abraham Maslow, whose hierarchy of needs I discussed in Chapter One, was the first to present an organized scale of all motivations, from the most basic to the most lofty. He listed survival as the most basic motivation, then a need for security, followed by a need to belong or to be loved. These are his "deficiency needs." For what he called "higher needs," he described self-esteem, self-actualization, and peak experience.

In the years since its publication, Maslow's hierarchy has inspired many attempts to develop motivation theory further, with psychologists, doctors, and scientists like R. B. Cattell, Ian Marshall, David Hawkins, and Daniel Goleman publishing more elaborate lists of motivations and different scales or hierarchies. These particular approaches pretty much correlate with one another. There are many, many others, but still no broad consensus among psychologists about the full range of human motivations nor which to emphasize. I have decided to use Marshall's scale in this book because it has evolved together with our joint work on spiritual intelligence, and it provides an essential insight into the way that a motivational shift can happen. Its close correlation with Cattell's list of motives grounds it in experimental psychology. This scale offers a new way of systematically diagnosing the motivational and emotional foundations of where a culture or an individual is now, and then suggests ways to shift the present state to a more desired future one. The diagnosis is made with emotional intelligence rather than traditional IQ, and shift occurs through applying spiritual intelligence.

The Scale of Motivations

Ian Marshall is a practicing medical psychiatrist and psychotherapist with a Jungian background and leaning. His Scale of Motivations, an earlier version of which was published in 1997, was derived from more than forty years of clinical observation of patient behavior and response.[1] As pictured below, it draws from Maslow's pyramid of needs, but extends Maslow's original six motivations to sixteen, eight positive ones and eight negative. These are arranged in a hierarchy from −8 to +8 and have the unique property that the positive and negative legs of the scale mirror one another. Thus +3, *power-within,* mirrors and is paired with −3, *craving;* +1, *exploration,* mirrors and is paired with −1 *self-assertion,* and so on. This has great implications for use of the scale.

As implied by the numbering, it is better to have a motive of +3 than one of −1, but it is also better to be at −1 than at −4. Our personal effectiveness increases, and our behavior improves or has a more positive outcome, as we progress up the scale. A leader driven by *fear* (−4) will adopt far more reactive and defensive strategies than a counterpart who is driven by *self-assertion* (−1). This has clear implications for risk management. *Fear* leads to behavior that is risk averse, or perhaps desperate; *self-assertion* may lead to overconfidence or carelessness.

In fact, not just our strategies but the even deeper cognitive processes underlying them alter as we move up or down the scale. It is clear that motivations drive behavior, but they also drive thinking. Each motivation is a whole paradigm, embracing assumptions, values,

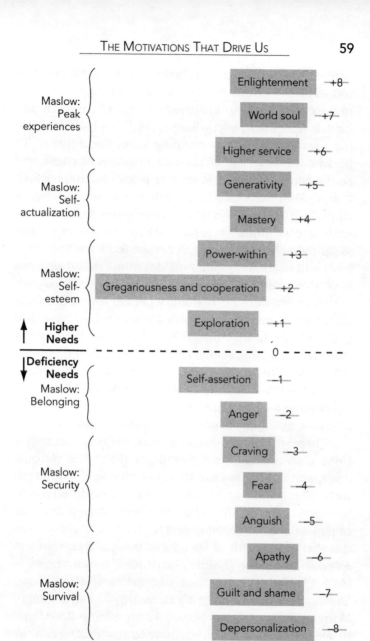

Figure 3.1 *Scale of Motivations*

aspirations, strategies, relationships, emotions, and behavior. It could be said of a paradigm what the philosopher Ludwig Wittgenstein said of tools: "If all I have is a hammer, everything looks like a nail." If I have the paradigm of fear, everything looks like a threat. To borrow the language of the new sciences of chaos and complexity (discussed at greater length in Chapter Six), a motivation acts as an "attractor" for our patterns of thought, just as the various numbered holes on the surface of a pinball machine act as attractors for the silver balls the player fires. A person motivated by *anger* (-2) will use a very different decision-making process from that used by one who is driven by *gregariousness and cooperation* $(+2)$. The angry person will be preoccupied with blame and a desire for retribution, and will seek strategies that bring this about, because everything that happens seems to be caused by an opponent or enemy. The cooperative person will be concerned with finding a balanced analysis of any problems and developing a consensus, seeing others as prospective partners, and appropriate strategies will follow.

Therefore any move up or down the scale of motivations also represents a paradigm shift. The visions, goals, and strategies (and therefore the results obtained by a corporation or a government or educational system) will be radically different depending upon those organizations' underlying motivations. It is clear from this that any growth or transformation process aimed at altering behavior (habits), attitudes, or emotions is bound to fail if it does not address motivations first. *Shifting motivation is the only stable way to shift behavior.* Motivations are causes; behaviors are effects. If we hope to see a shift from self-consuming to sustainable capitalism, we have to find some way to shift the corporate world's present driving motivations of *fear* (-4), *craving*

Seven Questions to Ask When Using the Scale of Motivations

1. What motivations drive us as individuals or as a culture in the present?
2. How do these motivations affect our behavior and strategies?
3. What results do we get?
4. Where would we like to be?
5. What motivations are needed to get there?
6. What do we need to do to make the motivational shift happen?
7. What kinds of behavioral and strategic changes will we see?

Questions 1 and 2 require the diagnostic skills of emotional intelligence; 4 and 5 will require spiritual intelligence. Question 3 requires a bit of each.

(−3), *anger* (−2), and *self-assertion* (−1), to the more positive ones of *exploration* (+1), *cooperation* (+2), *power-within* (+3), and *mastery* (+4). This is the momentous paradigm shift envisaged when I speak of creating spiritual capital, and the rest of this book is about making it happen.

Positive and Negative Mirroring

One further way to take advantage of the Scale of Motivations is to make diagnostic use of its positive and negative mirroring. Among other things, this mirroring (of +4 and −4, for instance) allows us to attach weight to the force of a motivation with respect to another motivation. Using it, we can derive by simple arithmetic whether the motivations of one individual or culture can contain those of another, or whether they will be overwhelmed by them in some positive or negative way.

An angry person (-2) can never contain another angry person. They just clash and make things worse. Nor can a cooperative person $(+2)$ have much effect on an angry person (-2). They just cancel each other out. However, an angry person's *anger* state (-2) can be raised by another person who is at least at $+3$, *power-within*. By the same token, an angry person (-2) can be dragged further down into *fear* (-4) by someone who is motivated by desperation (*anguish,* -5). This simple arithmetic lays the foundation for a new kind of motivational dynamics.

The arithmetic allows us to diagnose our relative position on the scale, and helps us to decide whether we can be of some use to another or to a situation, or whether we are simply threatened by them and need to disengage. This can enable us to evolve a strategy for how to handle the situation.

The positive and negative mirroring of the scale's motivations also allows us to identify what Jung would have called the "shadow" characteristics of any given motivation. Those are the characteristics we choose to disown or to project onto another because we can't bear to own them. The shadow is the "underside" or the "dark side" of a quality or personality trait. Thus *anger* (-2) is the shadow of *cooperation* $(+2)$; damnation (*depersonalization,* -8) the shadow of salvation (*enlightenment,* $+8$). Jung believed that an individual's or a culture's shadow provides an unconscious energy dynamic that greatly affects actual behavior. Our shadow haunts us and brings unwanted consequences. All the negative motivations on the scale are shadow motivations. That is, they result in self-defeating strategies. From the scale, it is clear that the four negative motivations that drive today's capitalism and business ethic mean that capitalism is living out of its own shadow. From there, it has inspired the same negative motivations in at least one of its enemies—terrorists, too, are driven by *fear, craving, anger,* and *self-assertion.*

Finding Ourselves on the Scale

Daniel Goleman has described self-awareness ("Recognizing a feeling as it happens") as the "keystone" of emotional intelligence.[2] He says that it is our primary required emotional competency. It is with honest, strong self-awareness that we must find our place on the Scale of Motivations. Yet this is more easily said than done. Because a motivation supports a whole paradigm—all our thoughts, perceptions, and assumptions—it is very difficult, if not impossible, for most individuals to diagnose their own position on the scale, especially if they are in some negative state. Self-awareness is the paramount competency of emotional intelligence, but it is also the most difficult to achieve.

Most of us live a tissue of lies, or at least illusions, and most of these are about ourselves or our group. Take the case of a global insurance company I once observed. This company had articulated its values as the "Four T's"—truth, trust, transparency, and teamwork. Employees basked in a feel-good factor about these values. They would have placed the company quite high on the scale, probably ranging from +1 to +4. Then one morning a senior executive came into the office and threw a suitcase full of women's garments around the office. They were his wife's. "He's been screwing her," he shouted, pointing at the CEO's private office. It turned out the CEO had been having an affair with the man's wife. To spend more time with her, he had promoted her beyond her competency to his personal assistant, and they frequently traveled abroad together on business trips. Employees now felt betrayed and saw the company values as a sham. The CEO's behavior had violated every one of the Four T's, and most people could now see that the company culture was really motivated by drives at -4 to -1.

People who work with paradigms argue that we can never see beyond our existing paradigm so long as it works. It is when a paradigm breaks down—as in the case of the Four T's—that its assumptions are exposed as false and we begin to look for a new paradigm. Traumatic incidents like that one can shake us out of our illusions. A betrayal, a dreadful crisis or failure, a significant loss can increase our self-awareness. Then, too, some people are above 0 on the Scale of Motivations, and we can gain a learning perspective on our own from their behavior. And many people who are at minus positions on the scale nonetheless have glimpses or twinges of higher motivations.

As Daniel Goleman has pointed out, being able interpret other people's emotions correctly and respond appropriately to them is also an important part of the diagnostic work of emotional intelligence. But we cannot properly interpret another's behavior or emotions if we do not know the true motives underlying the behavior. If we get these motives wrong, the strategies we devise in response to the other will be wrong.

The relationship between teenaged children and their parents is a familiar case of misinterpreted motives. Many parents, indeed probably most, relate to their children with motives at $+4$, *mastery,* or $+5$, *generativity* (loving creativity in the service of a higher cause). They want the best for their children and take an interest in their development. Sometimes this leads to nagging. But teenagers, with a newfound instinct for independence and motivated in this case by −4, *fear* (of being repressed), or −1, *self-assertion,* very often misinterpret their parents' motives as stemming from their own *self-assertion* (−1), *anger* (−2), or *fear* (−4) (of letting their children go). This leads to strategies of deceit and conflict on the part of the children, and often pushes the parents into defensive strategies.

According to David Hawkins, who constructed his own hierarchy of motivations based on assessing the degree of muscle tension associated with the attitudes accompanying various motivations (kinesiology), 85 percent of us are motivated by drives that score less than zero on the scale.[3] Of the 15 percent who score above 0, only about 4 percent ever get as high as +5, *creativity.* The vast majority, perhaps 60 percent, score between −4, *fear,* and −1, *self-assertion.* We have only to watch the behavior of most public figures, be they in business or politics, to see the alarming truth of this. On the more positive side, Hawkins reckons that the very few who act from higher motivations have a disproportionate capacity to drag the rest of us somewhat higher, or at least to make us aspire to higher motivations. Intellectual historians argue that all the progress ever made by humanity in its forty-thousand-year recorded history has been made through the leadership of the top 2 percent.

In my view, people or cultures whose motivational drives are below 0 can't really assess themselves (or others!) accurately. They can't listen to themselves because their negative paradigms skew all incoming data and give them blind spots. An increased self-awareness must come from being listened to or by holding a dialogue with others who are themselves motivated by at least +1, *exploration,* or +2, *cooperation.* Thus even finding ourselves on the Scale of Motivations requires that we work with others in dialogue or discussion groups. Conversations with disinterested but caring friends can help us assess some of our behavior, as of course can professional help—therapists, counselors, mentors, priests, or workshop leaders. The practice of 360-degree evaluation from colleagues and peers can also be very effective. In the next chapter I discuss each of the sixteen motivational states in turn and link them to characteristic behaviors and strategies which we can recognize clearly.

Apart from group work, the most effective method for an individual to reach a higher state of self-awareness is through some sort of meditation practice, for those who can engage in this effectively. Meditation takes the mind beyond the distractions and noise of the moment to a broader level of awareness that notices causes and patterns within events. In a meditative state, I can get beyond my anger to become aware that I am angry, and then reach a stage of reflection or insight as to its causes. Also, each of us has a number of barely conscious subpersonalities whose own split-off motivations might help or hinder us. "I" may be angry, though there may be a less accessible aspect of me that feels an underlying *power-within* or *mastery* associated with deep compassion. Through meditation it is possible to become conscious of these subpersonalities and thus better able to integrate them and their motivational drives.

Meditation transcends the whole level of ego awareness where motivations dwell, putting the mind more in touch with the deeper level of values that underlie motivations in the first place. This can move us from the diagnostic use of our emotional intelligence to the transformational use of our spiritual intelligence. We move from *recognizing* motivations to *shifting* them.

How We Move on the Scale

Once we see that we are acting from a lower motivation that has negative consequences, or we are inspired by a person or culture clearly acting from higher motivations than our own, we naturally want to know how to shift our own motivations. How can I get from thinking and acting out of −4, *fear,* to −2, *anger,* which is at least an improvement on my situation? If I am more ambitious, how can I move from −2, *anger,* to +2, *cooperation?* Or how can I prevent myself from being dragged down from +1, *exploration,* to −4, *fear?* In short, what are the dynamics of this scale of motivations and how does shift happen?

There are two kinds of shift that might happen to an individual or a culture with respect to the scale. The first is an external and most likely temporary or dependent, shift that can result from the influence of others or the environment. I may be in a state of *fear,* −4, and yet, finding myself surrounded by a group of people who are at *mastery,* +4, I may for a time become more self-confident. As a group, perhaps we can handle the threat. However, I will not really have addressed the underlying causes of my fearfulness and may fall back without the support of the masterful group.

Recent history provides a real case of individuals returning to their original motivations and attitudes once divorced from group pressure. The American GIs who were captured by the Chinese during the Korean War were brainwashed, and happily appeared on television criticizing capitalism and the United States. They had become "good communists." But within six months of being freed and living back in their familiar American environment, every one of them reverted to his earlier patriotic attitudes.

The second kind of possible shift is deeper, *internal,* and much more lasting. This results from examining original motives, coming to understand the purposes and values that underlie them, and then shifting those values themselves. The consequent motivational shift brings about a paradigm shift. This is the kind of motivational shift being sought in McKinsey Australia's spiritual intelligence leadership program, where the whole top two thousand employees of an organization are put through a program that assesses motivations and values.

I haven't yet laid the full groundwork to discuss internal, paradigm-shifting motivational change. That will require bringing spiritual intelligence into the discussion, which is the work of the next three chapters. But at this stage, it is already possible to see how environment or emotional intelligence influences how people can move up or down on the scale. This external dynamic can be articulated in four basic principles.

Principle One: A negative person or culture cannot help another on the negative scale. Two people stuck at *anger* (−2) will just spark each other off and make each other more angry. Two *assertive* people at −1 will get locked into a power struggle. Similarly, using a negative motivation to make a change in a situation can only result in getting to some other negative motivation. For instance, as noted in Chapter Two, Nike reacted out of *fear* (−4) to customer loss over sweatshops employing child labor in Southeast Asia. Its management changed company policy and offered their Asian workers better conditions. But this only brought company motivation one step higher, to *craving* (−3). They wanted to get profit back on track, and improving the conditions of their workers was just a necessary means toward that end.

Principle Two: A person at −3, *craving,* is just cancelled out by a person at +3, *power-within.* Equality of opposites is not enough to change the motivations of either person. To have the power to raise another up the scale, someone must make what chess players call a "knight's move." That is, it would take someone at +4, *mastery,* to raise a −3 to −2 or higher. This principle usually underlies the philosophy behind dialogue groups or mentoring—the notion that a dialogue facilitator or a mentor (or a workshop leader) is at a higher motivational level than the rest of the group and can thus raise the game.

Principle Three: An individual at +4 can contain another who is coming from −3; but an individual who is only at +2 can be dragged down by someone who is at −3. Thus a culture or a group higher up on the scale can raise the game for those lower down. This is the point of having priests, good teachers, master artisans, and servant leaders in society. They inspire us upward with their example or vision. But it is also the case that a culture can drag individuals down. Most children, for instance, begin at 0 on the scale in infancy but quickly move on to *exploration* (+1). They begin school filled with curiosity a sense of wonder. But much of the educational system is motivated by *fear* (−4) or *craving* (for control, −3). This very quickly reduces most children's educational experience to one of −3, a *craving* (for credentials), or worse still, −4, *fear* (of failure).

At a graduate business school in South Africa, an "idealism" survey was done on two groups of MBA students. The first group were young people just fresh out of university. They were found to be very idealistic in their work aspirations. They acted out of *exploration* (+1), *cooperation* (+2), and *power-within* (+3). They hoped to reach *mastery* (+4) through their MBA work. The second group were older MBA students who had worked in the corporate world for at least ten years. They were very low in idealism, filled with anger, and quite cynical. Ten years in a corporate culture whose driving motives are −4, *fear;* −3, *craving;* −2, *anger;* and −1, *self-assertion* had dragged these people down to its own level. *If we want to change the motives and behavior of people within corporate culture, we must change the underlying motivations of that culture itself.*

Principle Four: We can use our emotional intelligence (primarily self-awareness and emotional control) to move up the scale, provided this is accompanied by a wish not to hurt others or not to make a situation worse. For instance, if I know that I have a bad temper (−2, *anger*), I can make a great effort not to lose it. Now I am acting out of +2, *cooperation,* or perhaps even +3, *power-within* (self-mastery). But this kind of move begins to take us into the deeper territory of underlying values, and thus of spiritual intelligence. In this example, it is an underlying *value* of not wishing to cause harm that really shifts me to a higher motivation.

From now on I will focus on what spiritual intelligence is and does, and how using it can bring about a paradigmatic motivational shift. The shift from capitalism and business as we know it to spiritual capital requires such a shift. It requires raising the negative motivations that drive present business culture to higher, positive ones. But first, in the next chapter, I provide an outline of each of the sixteen motivations on the scale and an indication of the behavior and strategies to which it leads.

Applying the
Motivational Scale

The sixteen motivational states described on the scale are, as I said, "attractors" or whole paradigms that encompass behavior, emotions, attitudes, assumptions, values, thinking processes, and strategies. Thus to know the motivation or set of motivations driving individuals or whole cultures is to know a great deal about their internal state as well as how they will react with and influence their environment. It is to know the individual or organizational "psychology" and to be able to predict their approach to action—and its effectiveness.

We can assume from historical accounts of his past and his emotional reaction to Germany's humiliating defeat in World War One, and his own disastrous failure as an artist, for instance, that Adolf Hitler was motivated by *guilt and shame* (−7), *craving* (for power and glory, −3), *anger* (−2), and a good bit of *self-assertion* (−1). These motives were apparent in Hitler's speech and body language, as well as in the aggressive strategies he evolved. If world leaders had been able to see this during his rise to power, they would have had little difficulty believing that his *Reich* might pose a great threat to surrounding countries and to certain ethnic groups within Germany. Perhaps, seen at an earlier date, this would have allowed allied countries to counter Hitler's threat from a position of *power-within* (+3) or *mastery* (+4). Instead they waited until he began invading Austria and Poland, and then they responded from a position of *fear* (−4). Eleven million people died because they got it wrong.

This extreme example serves as a reminder that no good can come from negative motivations. As David Hawkins puts it, "All [motivational] levels below [0] are destructive of life in both the individual and society at large; all levels above [0] are constructive expressions of power."[1] A person or a culture must be at at least +1 to have a beneficial effect either personally or on the world. *The crises of capitalism are the crises of negative motivation.*

As I describe each of the motivations in turn, I do so in their positive and negative mirrored pairs. Thus I move up and down the scale simultaneously, letting each shadow—negative—motive come just after its positive equivalent. This is important for understanding the dynamics of internal shift when we come to that.

Familiar Motivations

The motives between +4 and −4, the most common, were all picked up by R.B. Cattell's statistical (factor analytic) studies of ordinary people. Beyond these limits is more the territory of genius and sainthood on one hand and of psychosis or nervous breakdown on the other. The vast majority of any working population will fall between +4 and −4.

0, Neutral

The position of neutrality is not itself a motivation. It is either our starting point as infants, or our life-changing crossover point from being driven by negative motivations to acting from more positive ones. It is like the neutral position in a car's clutch system, free and ready to go, but with no direction yet determined. Many of us awaken fresh in *neutral* each morning, before the memories, images, and emotions from the day before rush in to fill our consciousness. It is like the *tabula rasa* described by the philosopher Descartes—the tablet on which nothing is yet written.

+1, Exploration

Exploration is associated with curiosity, a sense of wonder, and an open, willing attitude to whatever life throws in our path. It is very common in young children. It reflects a desire to know our way about a scene or a situation, such as that first exploration we do when we arrive at a new tourist or residential destination. People with this motivation are in open dialogue with their environment; they look and listen and they easily engage. *Exploration* is a recognition that we need to know, to learn, to explore, and that it will be fulfilling to do so. It involves us in reading books, papers, and magazines—anything that will teach us more and allow us to engage with our environment actively. It makes us good students and willing, attentive employees. People driven by this motivation are usually interested in music, art, and film. They love traveling to new places and are enthusiastic about solving new problems or meeting new challenges. They like to know how things work, and they pursue knowledge and learning for their own sake. All their strategies will be bent on reaching out, on extending their skills, knowledge, or area of activity. They will be drawn to innovation because it excites them, and they will greet adverse circumstances with a "What can I make of this?" attitude.

− 1, Self-Assertion

This motivation is associated with thoughtlessness, unbridled competitiveness, too much pride, self-centeredness, and aggression. David Hawkins comments that there is enough energy in this motivation to drive the U.S. Marine Corps. Like the Marines, self-assertive people are always charging over some hill, imposing their will and structure on the environment, "taking no prisoners." In business, they set out to conquer the market and destroy the competition. Their attitude toward learning and knowledge is manipulative. They try to assert what they already know, or they engage in learning as a means of strengthening their already entrenched position. Thus they are not open to learning things that do not further their ends. In the end, this is self-defeating. Self-assertive people have a will to power that brings them into conflict with anyone who has a strong or independent point of view different from theirs. Having two self-assertive people or cultures in conflict makes for war, psychological or real. They are argumentative and averse to dialogue and must have their own way. Self-assertive people are also driven by a need for status and self-esteem of a sort dependent on others. They need the good opinion or open admiration of others. They care how they dress and dress to win further esteem. They will adopt strategies that gain them territory or acclaim or that boost their power. They play to win, and count the scalps of the losers. They can be pleasant, but only if they are getting their own way and receiving enough respect.

+2, Gregariousness and Cooperation

We human beings are social animals. We need to relate to others and usually gain great nourishment from doing so. Some psychologists call this tendency our "herd instinct," but that phrase dismisses the reality without valuing it properly. The bonds that we form with our fellows and culture through our gregariousness are bonds of fierce loyalty often based on shared values as well as shared goals. Gregarious people usually seek company, preferring it to being alone. They like people and enjoy doing shared social or work-related activities in company.

People motivated by *gregariousness and cooperation* make good team members and have a strong esprit des corps. But the stronger aspect of this motive is the drive toward cooperation that is required if we are to be with others. This causes us to evolve strategies of pleasing, negotiation, conciliation, and conflict management. Cooperative people are good at seeing the other's point of view, and they harbor a natural respect for it even if they disagree. This makes them very good negotiators who are also good at drawing out creative ideas in others. They are good listeners. Gregarious and cooperative people usually seek social occupations, and are common among professions like teaching, coaching, and social work. They are the social "glue" of any group or organization, always evolving strategies that would bring people together. Every new relationship looks like a new opportunity. The motives of +1 and +2, taken together, are sufficient for living in a small group, in a static way. But evolution and creativity require higher motivation.

−2, Anger

We all recognize *anger* in others. Angry people are usually very cold, carefully holding their emotions in check, or very hot, letting their anger spew all over the place. They feel bad and they blame someone or something for that feeling. Bad things in life are someone's fault. As David Hawkins puts it, "Anger as a lifestyle is exemplified by irritable, explosive people who are oversensitive to slights and become 'injustice collectors,' quarrelsome, belligerent, or litigious."[2] They are often rebellious just for the sake of rebelling. Angry people seldom feel like cooperating. Where cooperative people seek company and thus the resolution of conflict, angry people often reject the group or society. They feel spiteful and seek strategies of revenge. The other is the enemy, and the enemy must be punished or conquered. Vandalism is driven by *anger,* as is terrorism. Both vandals and terrorists feel overlooked or excluded by society. Their need for self-esteem is threatened or frustrated and they want to lash out with a claim that their existence (cause, values, or whatever) be recognized. Indeed, frustration of one sort or another underlies most *anger:* love or loyalty that has not been requited, worth that has not been valued, a point of view that has not been heard, a self that has been rejected, denied, or left out. As a business strategy, *anger* leads to finding some way to beat, destroy, or damage the competition, even if cooperation might have led to a better result. In an executive, it can lead to strategies of finding fault.

The famous "dirty tricks" campaign British Airways ran against Virgin Atlantic was a strategy inspired by a wish to destroy or damage the competition. BA telephoned passengers intending to fly on Virgin and offered them cheaper fares if they would transfer to BA.

+3, Power-Within

We usually associate personal power with the ability to move or dominate others: *power-over*. But power-over is external power. A person has it by virtue of owning something, occupying some position of authority or influence, having a strong body, "being somebody." People acting from −1, *self-assertion* seek power-over as a means of using others to make themselves feel strong or important. Unless wielded from a higher motivation, most power-over usually creates winners and losers, and conflict results.

The only person the man or woman motivated by *power-within* really seeks to have power-over is himself or herself. These are people who are centered in themselves, at peace with themselves. They know whom they love and what they value and they act from this level of love and values. They have *integrity* in the strict sense that they are whole people, as well as showing behavior that is filled with integrity. They may also be rooted in their skills, or, if they are athletes, in their well-trained minds and bodies. The very pleasurable sense of "flow" when performing at our physical or mental best is the correlate of *power-within*.[3]

People who have *power-within* are trustworthy. We know where they are coming from and know that that is from a place within themselves that we can trust. They have a recognizable personal style derived from deeper commitments, and they have a strongly felt sense of their own identity. These people can be counted on to fulfill any responsibility they take on. They often act from a sense of responsibility, of loyalty, service, or guardianship (stewardship), though they can say no if they disagree. They are more self-directed than other-directed, and think quite independently. Since their deepest motivation is a sense of their own values and direction, they are open to and tolerant of the ways and values of others. They are open to diversity and will often evolve strategies that bring many different elements or voices together. If in positions of power-over (as parents, as executives), their strategy will include empowering others. They will listen to all sides before making a decision, and seldom rush to judgment. Their strategies are usually driven by a quiet (sometimes fierce) determination. They get things done.

−3, Craving

The Buddha said that craving is the root of all suffering. Most of the Seven Deadly Sins are sins of craving. *Craving* expresses itself as perpetual restlessness, a sense of never having enough, of there always being something more to want or need. Driven by a sense of inner emptiness (the exact opposite of *power-within*), these people constantly adopt strategies of grasp-ing. They are greedy people, like Erisychthon, people who are never satisfied. Most feel they "are owed," that some-one, somewhere didn't give them what they needed or never gave them a break. They want things, but often they don't think they should have to pay for them. Their greed makes them materialistic if it is a greed for money or things and it makes them jealous if it is a hunger to be loved. Capitalist greed is a greed for ever more profit, and damn the consequences.

Craving makes us jealous because we see, in what-ever someone else has, something we want. *Craving* is of course the basis of all addictions—overeating, gambling, alcoholism, drug addiction, and the rest—and the strate-gies of the craving person are always the strategies of an addict: A quick fix rather than a long-term plan, instant results rather than patient plodding or planning, seeking out feel-good factors or "highs," betraying anything or anyone (including ourselves) that frustrates satisfaction. Craving people may not be trustworthy where the object of their craving is concerned, and they are often deeply irresponsible.

+4, Mastery

The man or woman (or culture) that has reached +3, *power-within,* is centered in deep personal values. But when our motivation reaches *mastery,* we find ourselves rooted in wider interpersonal values and skills— especially those of a profession, a tradition, or a system of understanding distinctive of wider thinking or some shared vision. A master stonemason wields with his hammer all the skill and all the power of master stonemasons throughout history. He draws on his craft's collective pool of wisdom and skill. A master-level executive leads with an easy air of authority and inner self-assurance, applying an *instinct* for good strategies and decisions. A master's behavior and decisions always show a sense of inner discipline and of "flow." This is developed and directed by reining in whim and easy desires or snap decisions through disciplines like meditation or prayer, or through constant practice of a skill or an art. At the level of *mastery,* we see the bigger picture or are in tune with a larger pattern, and thus our strategies are more complex and look to the longer term. We'll seek long-term objectives and constantly reframe those objectives as we take in new information. Because we are in touch with a wider pool of potentiality through being grounded in the collective wisdom of our tradition, we will see opportunities and possible innovations where others don't. The martial art of

Aikido develops *power-within;* Shao-Lin Kung Fu, featured in the recent Chinese film *Crouching Tiger, Hidden Dragon,* is more a practice of masters. The Aikido warrior moves with a sense of personal power, the Shao-Lin master with a power "granted by the gods."

David Hawkins claims that very few people in our culture get above the level of *mastery.* Only 8 percent to 10 percent achieve mastery. We find among them most people who have reached the top level of their profession or craft—senior doctors, higher executives, first violin players in major orchestras, champion athletes, leading (but not great) scientists. Winston Churchill and Franklin Delano Roosevelt were master politicians, Marie Curie was a master scientist.

−4, Fear

Fear is associated with anxiety, suspicion, a sense of being threatened or of being too vulnerable. It is the very opposite of being master of the situation. Acting from this motive, I seek always to protect or defend myself. I see others in my environment as threats or enemies. I tend to see opportunities or challenges as possible threats (because I doubt my ability to deal with them). I tend to withdraw from people (those I feel threaten me) or the environment, and I become timid. My body language is defensive, and I avoid taking the initiative or calling attention to myself. I don't volunteer and I don't take risks. *Fear* isolates me from the moment and costs me my spontaneity. Hence the expression, "frozen with fear." The strategies I adopt will always be reactive and cautious. They will be ones of avoidance and retreat, or they may be passive. Not wanting to rock the boat or draw attention to myself, I may act so as to hide my true emotions or aspirations. And I may take unnecessary precautions to avoid being blamed or criticized. The battery of unnecessary tests and procedures ("defensive medicine") for which American medicine is famous stems from this fearful strategy. Driven by *fear,* business executives become risk-averse and closed to any kind of innovation or exploration.

Advanced Motivations

We get to a place with the next eight motivations where we begin to find the exceptional people, either the supernormal and especially gifted or the subnormal and especially injured or damaged. These are the realms of greatness at the one extreme and of psychiatric illness at the other. No more than 4 percent of the general population is driven by these higher or lower motives. These are the people whose personalities differ from the norm, perhaps up to the extreme of incipient madness— borderline manic-depressive (bipolar) individuals, or those individuals prone to but not actually in schizophrenic breakdown, who are known as *schizotypal.* There is a well-recognized correlation between this "borderline madness" and creativity. The same qualities that give rise to unusual behavior confer unusual vision or exceptionally sensitive temperament. For such personalities, the risks of great catastrophe are balanced by the chance of great genius.

We don't see many of these people at the positive end, but their presence in a culture is necessary to raise the motivational level of others lower down the scale. Only someone who is at least at +5, *generativity,* or at +6, *higher service,* can raise another would-be leader from +3 *power-within,* to +4, *mastery.* Such higher-motivated individuals are also necessary to raise the motivational level of a culture, because it is they who bring in the creativity and freshness of new energy. It is among the positive ones of them that we will hope to find the "new Knights Templar" of corporate generativity and service (see Chapter Ten).

+5, Generativity

Generativity is a special manifestation of creativity. It is creativity driven by love or passion. It stands in what Martin Buber would have called an *I-thou* relationship to the medium of its output. A painter *loves* color and the practice of art. Albert Einstein said that he loved mathematics; Isaac Newton felt a great awe and love for the universe he wished to explore. This love or passion gives generative people a sense of playfulness about their creativity. They *enjoy* it and identify with it. The work is the life. The story that the chemist Friedrich Kekule dreamt his ground-breaking image of the benzene ring is famous. But it is less well known that in Kekule's dream, the six carbon atoms that made up the ring were holding hands and dancing. Kekule had a child's sense of fun about his work.

Because their creativity is so closely linked to play, generative people are often generative in many directions. They just spark off creativity, and are excited by anything that arouses their interest or curiosity. So their creativity is not necessarily in service to anything. It is just driven by an unbounded love. The strategies they adopt are always strategies of learning or discovery. They are playful strategies—seeing what will happen "if," and delighting in it whatever it is. They readily take risks.

Masters (+4) draw out the potentiality within their shared tradition. They are the leading expressers *of* a tradition. Generative people create *new* traditions, new paradigms. They love and are drawn to the unknown or the unexplored and their creative gifts allow them to give new shape to the unformed. The German poet Rilke would have called them "the bees of the invisible," restlessly gathering the nectar that becomes the visible for others. Most of the very great names that we remember from human intellectual and artistic history were people motivated by generativity, from Plato to Picasso. Very great scientists like Newton or Einstein were driven by generativity, as are some of today's great businessmen. Steve Jobs at Apple Computer was one, Konosuke Matsushita who created Japan's electricity industry, Henry Ford, probably Bill Gates and certainly Virgin's Richard Branson are a few others. Branson is a particularly good example of *generativity* at work because his boyish creativity sparks off in many different directions. He lists "having fun" as one of Virgin's core company values.

−5, Anguish

Hamlet's famous soliloquy, "To be or not to be, that is the question," is the cry of an anguished man. Unlike grief or mourning, the necessary and healthy reaction to loss, *anguish* arises from a sense of being lost or helpless for what to do or what to decide. It comes from a sense of blocked potential. The generative process itself is blocked. We wring our hands and feel despair. We feel stuck, caught in the moment, with little prospect for movement. *Anguish* often results from incurable tragedy—having a damaged child, being an athlete who has lost physical agility, or being infertile and desperately wanting children. Retirement can bring it on, or immersion in a situation that we feel we can't handle.

Anguished people have no strategies because their very anguish arises from the fact that they can see no strategies. Everything seems impossible. This is, of course, an important component of depression. But although people living with *anguish* are suffering, they have not lost all hope, as is the case with −6, *apathy*.

+6, Higher Service

Higher service is the motive that drives the servant leader, the highest and most dedicated form of leadership possible. All great leaders serve something from beyond themselves, but the servant leaders, or "knights" as I think of them, serve transpersonal values—things like goodness, justice, truth, the alleviation of suffering, the salvation or enlightenment of others. All leaders serve their fellows, their community, their country or company, but servant leaders ultimately serve their own notion of the highest or most sacred. The best of them serve that longing in the human soul that conjures up visions and possibilities. They have a sense of vocation, of being called to serve, and in answering to this they find their own deepest peace, their own destiny. This is *focused* creativity, going beyond +5.

Servant leaders, or knights, make things happen that others have found impossible, they create new ways for human beings to relate to one another, new ways for companies to serve society, new ways for societies to *be*. The Buddha, Moses, and Jesus were such leaders. In our own times we have had the good fortune to be served by Gandhi, Martin Luther King Jr., Mother Teresa, Nelson Mandela, and the Dalai Lama. But there is no need for such greatness in servant leadership. Any of us can be a servant leader if we act from the motive of higher service.

Servant leaders necessarily deal with power, but they do so through humility and personal surrender. Power is always used to further the good they serve, never to aggrandize themselves. As Jesus said, "Not my will, Lord, but thine." For the enterprising and very determined personality types who naturally become leaders, such surrender is not easy. Its very possibility is an act of grace.

The strategies adopted by servant leaders will often be bold and large scale. They will be canny strategies that recognize the best and the worst in people and know how to use both to further the cause. They usually have a panoramic vision of the possible, like Gandhi's dream of Indian independence and the nonviolent path to achieving it or King's dream of a society freed from racism.

The nineteenth-century Indian philosopher Vivekenanda said, "This universe is just a gymnasium in which the soul is taking exercise." Vivekenanda was one of those who inspired Gandhi's view of "trusteeship," his own particular vision of servant leadership. Ghandi said that when an individual or a company obtains more than their proportionate share of the world's wealth they should become a trustee of that portion for God's people. This is the vision we now need a critical mass of business leaders to adopt if we are to move from capitalism as usual to spiritual capital.

− 6, Apathy

If Hamlet is the man of *anguish,* Macbeth is the man reduced to *apathy.* "Tomorrow and tomorrow and tomorrow/Creeps in this petty pace from day to day,/To the last syllable of recorded time/ And all our yesterdays have lighted fools/The way to dusty death . . . [Life] is a tale/ Told by an idiot, full of sound and fury,/Signifying nothing." Macbeth has seen all his dreams and schemes come to nothing and now he feels that he is nothing. He is the embodiment of the existentialist philosopher Sartre's "Man is a useless passion."

In *apathy* we are overwhelmed with a sense of *anomie,* of having no role to play in life. Where the person of *anguish* suffers as a result of being unable to play life's game, the person of *apathy* can't see that there is any game to play. Apathetic people have very little energy, only barely enough to keep going. They show little interest in anything and often neglect themselves and their affairs. They adopt no strategies because nothing seems worthwhile. This is a very deep form of depression. It may be the norm for Third World people who are just at or only slightly above survival level.

+7, World Soul

The servant leaders at +6 is rooted in their "God," but their calling is to be of service in this world of daily affairs. At the next level up, +7, *world soul,* people see themselves, others, and nature as parts of the divine made manifest. If habitual, this state may be accompanied by a withdrawal from the world of daily life, as with monks and some artists. These people, perhaps only one in ten million of the population, commune with a world of archetypes and pure forms. They see the world bathed in celestial light (Wordsworth), or are inspired by the voices of angels (the poet Rilke). They have lost the craving to be themselves, the sense of ego, and hence the sense of limitation. They dwell at, or sometimes reach, a level of awareness that transcends space and time and thus have a sense of immortality, of the infinite. Their consciousness has become one with the collective unconscious of our species (and sometimes that of other species) and when they do speak or create works of art it is as though through these utterances we hear the voice of the collective unconscious. Mozart's music was literally dictated from this level. He said that he merely wrote down what he heard. Dante's vision of both the Inferno and of Paradise comes from these realms of the divine and archetypal. So, too, does Shakespeare's genius for seeing and bringing to life the disparate points of view in a complex array of human characters. "All the world's a stage, and all men and women merely players," and Shakespeare saw them from the vantage point of a celestial playwright.

Most of us will never reach this mystical level of motivation as a stable state, and indeed would not aspire to do so, but at least half of us do have intimations of it through occasional (or once-in-a-lifetime) mystical experiences of oneness, beauty, peace, or love. We also gain intimations of it through the great works of the geniuses who dwell there, and this is why art, music, and literature are so necessary to the human soul.

For people at +7, motivation is toward celebrating the divine aspect of the world, and thus toward any strategies that further that cause. Distractions will be painful or indeed beyond being heeded, as these people's calling is to a world beyond the world. Some people enter this realm prematurely, as an escape from worldly problems. Their worldly personalities are often immature or damaged, and many of the great among them have ended their lives in early death or madness.

−7, Shame and Guilt

Shame and guilt fill a person with an almost exactly opposite sense of being to that experienced by *world soul*. When overcome by the motivations of −7, I feel wholly *apart* from any meaningful or deeper level of reality. Indeed, I feel out of joint with existence—that I have no right to be here, or that my presence in some way makes the world a worse place. I experience myself as a wound or a scar on the face of existence, and may wish to destroy myself. I simply cannot face myself or go on living with my guilt.

Death rates are high among people driven from this motivation, who often resort to ritual suicide. The Japanese tradition of hara-kiri results from loss of face (that is, *shame and guilt*), as did the practice of disgraced Roman generals' falling on their swords. Judas killed himself out of unbearable shame. People acting from this level have sometimes betrayed their own deepest ideals, and their strategies may be ones of self-destruction—either directly through suicide or indirectly through drugs, alcoholism, or reckless behavior. But violently aggressive or grandiose strategies may result if the *shame and guilt* have resulted from humiliation. Humiliation can also result in strategies to harm others, to gain vengeance against them for real or imagined slights, or to find scapegoats who can be blamed for our unbearable pain. As noted, Hitler had *shame and guilt* as one of his driving motivations. We are, here, at the gate of evil.

+8, Enlightenment

We come at this point almost to a failure of words or images. As Lao-tzu wrote at the opening of the *Tao-te Ching*, "The way that can be expressed in words is not the eternal way." That small handful of people in human history who have reached *enlightenment* and written about it can only allude, or speak in metaphor. They speak commonly of the total absorption or annihilation of self in "the Absolute" or "the nothingness." The

Christian mystic St. John of the Cross described it in these terms in "Upon a Dark Night":

> All things I then forgot,
> My cheek on Him who for my coming came.
> All ceased, and I was not,
> Leaving my cares and shame
> Among the lilies, and forgetting them.

That the Absolute is described in so many mystical traditions as an emptiness or a darkness follows from our inability to grasp it with concepts or images. As St. John says, "It is a lightsome darkness and a rich naught." The Buddhists describe it (*Shunyata*) as "an emptiness that is full." Even quantum physics has a vision of the absolute ground state of reality, which it calls "the quantum vacuum." Again, the quantum vacuum is empty only of structure and qualities; it is replete with possibilities. We must "grasp" (be absorbed within them) these naught absolutes in a state of structureless awareness.

It is possible to have experienced *enlightenment* and then to have returned to the world. The Buddha did so, as did those who have written about their experiences. But the return to the world is as an altered person, free of all negative motivations and partially identified with the experienced divine reality. As St. Paul said after his conversion, "Now there lives, not I, but Christ living in me." Or we have in T. S. Eliot's *Four Quartets* the thought, "Below, the boar hound and the boar, Pursue their pattern as before, But reconciled among the stars." Back in the world, these people live lives of grace. They are at peace with themselves and existence. Though they may pass as quite ordinary, the ordinary is for them exalted by an inner light.

−8, Depersonalization

A person who has reached *enlightenment* is all inner light without physical shell. A person who has undergone *depersonalization* is an empty shell with no core. Here, the sense of "I" has disappeared because the ego self has disintegrated. There is no "person" left, only random utterances and uncoordinated behavior. This is the inner world of the hospitalized schizophrenic or the hopelessly burnt-out alcoholic or drug addict. This is as close as we get to damnation while still alive. There is no further disintegration beyond it but death itself.

Shifting Our Motivations

These sixteen positive and negative motivations are states in which we become fixed. But the whole point of the Scale of Motivations (and of this book) is to show that no one need stay fixed, or stuck. It is possible to shift our motivations, either upward or downward. Upward motivation requires that we pump psychic energy into our system; downward shift happens when a situation or an underlying belief or value system drains us of this energy. My goal in this book is to stress the possibility and the necessity of upward shift. To understand the dynamics of this, it is essential to look more closely at the role played by spiritual intelligence (SQ) in our lives and decision-making processes.

5

SQ—Spiritual Intelligence

Mats Lederhausen first contacted me a few years ago when I was about to visit Sweden. He told me that he had read my books, and that he had a problem he wanted to discuss. He asked if we could meet. At the time, Mats was the chief executive of McDonald's for Sweden.

We met in a café on the outskirts of Stockholm. Mats was in his mid-thirties, dark, handsome, and in obvious good health. He seemed nervous at first, slightly embarrassed by his reason for wanting to see me. "I suppose you could say," he began, "that I have a 'spiritual problem.' I am still young, I have a beautiful family and plenty of money, and I'm at the top of my profession here in Sweden. But I'm not happy. I feel there has to be something more that I could be doing with my life. I'm not certain that I'm on the right path doing the job that I do." Mats said that he felt deeply concerned about the state of the world, particularly the environmental crisis facing the globe and the breakdown of community. "Big companies like McDonald's," he added, "aren't doing enough to face these things." He came from a Jewish family and had been taught as a boy that a man must take some responsibility for society. "Yet what am I doing?" he asked. "I'm making money. I spend ten to twelve hours of my day working for McDonald's, and I'm not serving any of the things I deeply care about. I want to make a difference. Want, if you like, to use my life to serve. But I don't know how. I just know that I want to be part of the solution. Not the problem." Mats feared he was letting himself down and being a poor role model for his children.

"I suppose I can see three options for myself," he continued. "I can stay on at McDonald's and hope to rise to a position of power within the company where I could leverage the changes I would like to see. But that's probably not very likely. I could leave McDonald's and become an independent consultant trying to encourage other companies to make big changes. But then, nobody really listens to consultants. Or, in extreme, I suppose I could just go off to a Tibetan monastery and meditate." Mats said colleagues in the United States accused him of having caught "the Tibetan virus," and that he should just ease his conscience as they did by giving to charity or by working with young people on weekends. "But that's not enough for me," he concluded. "I want to use my *professional* life to make a difference. What should I do?"

The unease Mats felt, his concern, and his deep need to do something about making his life serve some meaningful purpose are all signs of what I call his high "spiritual intelligence." It is an intelligence that causes him to wrestle with questions of meaning and value and that prods him to want to engage his life with some kind of service to some higher or deeper cause. This is the intelligence of the conscience, the intelligence that provides the human sense of morality and a further sense of the sacred, a sense that life has a deeper dimension than the mere "getting and spending" of daily activity. Mats didn't use the actual words, but I think that he wants to use his life in business to build spiritual capital. His spiritual intelligence is a necessary part of his possibility of doing so.

Scientists define *intelligence* as the ability to solve problems and the ability to create strategies or to fashion tools that are useful for reaching goals. If your goal is to make a lot of money, your intelligence allows you to form a strategy for how to do so. If your goal is to improve the plight of humanity, your intelligence may lead you to adopt quite a different strategy for doing that.

Whether we choose to make money or to improve the plight of humanity is, however, a matter of our *values,* and until very recently values have not been thought to bear on intelligence. Values were regarded as horribly subjective, intelligence as something measurable and objective. Today we know better. How can we intelligently choose one life goal or strategy in preference to another if we do not use our values as a criterion? The paradox raised by that question is now leading intelligence theorists to say that serving values is an aspect of human intelligence after all. This blows wide open our whole understanding of what intelligence includes, and raises the likelihood that there is more than one kind of intelligence.

This new intelligence debate raises the question of whether different intelligences are in play when we set out to create different kinds of capital. Does making money (material capital) require a different intelligence from that needed to build strong relationships and trust and to serve the community (social capital)? And does a wish to improve the plight of humanity (spiritual capital) require a whole third kind of intelligence? If so, how do we recognize and choose which to employ in given circumstances, which to nurture and grow?

Three Kinds of Intelligence

From the beginning of the twentieth century, human intelligence was equated with *IQ*, the Intelligence Quotient. Psychologists at that time devised a test that could measure individuals' IQ scores, and these tests were used to sift out the brightest and the best. They were used originally by the U.S. Army to choose officer material, but later came into general use by universities and employers to distinguish potential high-flyers. During the course of the century, taking an IQ test at various points during the education and job-seeking process became a universal practice. We have all taken one at some point.

An IQ score measures certain basic and largely inherited (it was believed) spatial, numerical, and linguistic abilities, but because it was the only measurable intelligence indicator available, it was taken as a mark of a person's full intelligence. It is rare for an IQ score to change much during the course of a life.

By the 1960s, IQ tests and scores became very controversial. First of all, it was realized by then that the test was measuring a particular kind of intelligence—rational, logical, linear intelligence, the kind of intelligence used to solve certain kinds of logical problems and to do certain kinds of strategic thinking. It is the kind of intelligence nurtured by Western school systems, and it has dominated Western business. Second, the multicultural awareness of the 1960s caused psychologists to notice that different ethnic groups and different genders scored differently or erratically on the IQ test. Either, they had to conclude, something was wrong with the test, or else people of different ethnicity, race, or gender had different levels of intelligence. Both options were controversial, but the IQ test was at that time the only definition or measure of intelligence available.

It was only in the mid-1990s that Daniel Goleman's book on "emotional intelligence" (EQ) changed the whole intelligence paradigm.[1] Goleman's writing was based on research work at top American universities by neuroscientists who noted that human emotions are an important factor in human intelligence. If our emotions are healthy and mature, and there is no associated brain damage, we use whatever IQ we have more effectively. If, however, the emotions are damaged or immature, or there is damage to the brain's emotional center, then we may not use whatever IQ we possess either wisely or appropriately. If the mechanisms with which we *feel* are damaged, we *think* less effectively. This is obvious in the common-sense case of the classic "absent-minded professor" who is brilliant at some intellectual subject, but who cannot tie his own shoelaces. The contrary is also evident in people of supposedly lower intelligence (lower IQ) who happen to be very gifted in working with people.

Emotional intelligence is an intelligence associated with how well we relate to and understand other people and the situations within which we encounter them. It is also associated with our ability to understand and manage our own emotions of fear, anger, aggression, or resentment. As Goleman said, "If we can't control such emotions, they will control us." Goleman went on to define EQ as our ability to assess or recognize the situation we are in, to read other people's and our own emotions, and to behave appropriately.

The work that Goleman wrote about revolutionized our understanding of intelligence and was quickly seen to have practical application in general life and in the workplace. Unlike IQ, which remains pretty much steady throughout life, EQ can be nurtured and improved. We can *learn* to behave more intelligently with other people or in recognizing and dealing with our own emotions. EQ also broadened out somewhat our notion of strategic thinking because it became evident that people pursue emotional strategies as well as rational ones, or at least that there is often an emotional contribution to the strategies we form. But EQ was not the last word in intelligence research.

Toward the end of the 1990s, neurological research suggested that the brain has a whole third "Q" or kind of intelligence. This is the intelligence with which we have access to deep meaning, fundamental values, and a sense of abiding purpose in our lives, and the role that this meaning, values, and purpose play in our lives, strategies, and thinking processes. This is the intelligence Mats Lederhausen was exhibiting in his concern to make his life serve some deep purpose. I called this third Q "SQ," for "spiritual intelligence."[2] SQ makes us ask the big questions: Why was I born? What is the meaning of my life? Why am I devoting my life to this relationship or this job or this cause? What am I really trying to achieve with this project or with my life? It allows us to see the larger context in which events take place and to see the big picture. It gives our lives an overarching canopy of meaning and value.

As noted earlier, *spiritual* comes from the Latin word *spiritus,* meaning the vitalizing principle of an organism. The "S" in SQ could also be derived from the Latin word *sapientia* (Greek *sophia*), meaning "wisdom"—wisdom intelligence. SQ embraces all that we traditionally mean by wisdom, as opposed to mere knowledge acquisition or to a rather mechanistic talent for solving problems.

Artists, mystics, great men and women of all faiths and of no faith remind us that there is a transpersonal source that exceeds the boundaries of human description. People motivated by *generativity* (+5), or the even higher motivations of *higher service, world soul,* or *enlightenment,* have considerable access to this dimension. Our spiritual intelligence gives us all a glimmer of this infinite or sacred realm, an opportunity to hear the whispers of angels or to make brushing contact with archetypal energies. It puts us in touch with something larger than ourselves, with the incomprehensible that lends meaning and significance to the finite in our own lives. Psychological surveys have shown that at some time in our adult lives, 50–70 percent of us have consciously felt such a brush with the infinite, experienced as an intimation of overwhelming beauty, profound love, deep truth, or an awe-inspiring sense of the unity of all things.

It is important to stress once again that the use of the word *spiritual* in relation to intelligence has no necessary connection with institutional religion. A person may be high in SQ but have no religious faith or belief of any kind. Equally, a person may be very religious but low in SQ. Religion is based on particular set of customs, beliefs and values, like being a Christian, Muslim, or Jew. Which, if any, religion we follow usually depends upon culture and upbringing. SQ, by contrast is an *innate* capacity of the human brain—it is based on structures in the brain that give us that basic ability to form meanings, values, and beliefs in the first place. SQ is *pre-cultural,* and more primary than religion. It is because we have spiritual intelligence in the first place that humanity later evolved religious systems as answers to the questions that SQ makes us ask.

Spiritual intelligence is "the soul's intelligence." It is the intelligence that makes us whole, that allows us to integrate the many fragments of our lives, activities, and being. It allows us to know what we and our organizations are *about*. SQ puts us in touch with the depths of our being and with the deep wells of our potentiality. It allows insights and understanding to move from those depths to the surface of our being where we act, think, and feel. Indeed, this is my personal understanding of what it means to have a soul in the first place—to be a living channel through which life's deeper dimensions and potentialities can rise to the surface and enter the world. It is our spiritual intelligence that gives us (or makes us into!) a soul.

SQ also helps us to evolve. More than just sustaining the known or the given, SQ takes us into the unknown and into the could-be. It allows us to aspire to higher motivations and enables us to act from these. In the evolution of our human species, it was the quest for meaning that triggered our brains to evolve language. In the evolution of society, our quest for meaning and deep values has caused us to select out (over time, and with many mistakes!) the best leaders for our groups, the leaders who most inspire us to dream or to stretch ourselves. Our SQ's search for ever greater meaning, purpose, and value makes us *dissatisfied* with the given, inspiring us to create ever more of what we seek. That, too, it pushes us to grow and develop as a culture.

Finally, SQ provides us with a kind of unboundaried insight into and understanding of the *whole* of a situation, a problem, or into the whole of existence itself. It gives us a deep sense of *knowing* or of *discovering* the deepness or significance of things. In *The Tibetan Book of Living and Dying,* for instance, Sogyal Rinpoche describes the deep impact on his consciousness and the vast implications for his life that resulted from his grasping, in a moment of insight, the true nature of impermanence. But what he says here about impermanence can apply to any deep insight gained through SQ.

> It is as if all our lives we have been flying in an airplane through dark clouds and turbulence, when suddenly the plane soars above these into a clear boundless sky. We are inspired and exhilarated by this emergence into a new dimension of freedom. . . . And as this new awareness begins to become vivid and almost unbroken, there occurs what [ancient Hindu writings] call a "turning about in the seat of consciousness," a personal, utterly non-conceptual revelation of what we are, why we are here, and how we should act. This "amounts in the end to nothing less than a new life, a new birth, you could say a resurrection."[3]

SQ: Our Paradigm-Making and Paradigm-Breaking Intelligence

IQ is a formal intelligence that learns how to manipulate and use formal rules, like the rules of grammar or the rules of arithmetic. It always works *within* a set of rules. By this definition, personal computers are high in IQ, but they can operate only within their programming. If we want them to do something outside the program, someone has to rewrite it.

EQ, as defined by Goleman, is essentially an adaptive intelligence. We read the situation we are in and we behave "appropriately" in order to adapt to it. It is a part of our EQ that we can read the conventions (emotional and social rules) of the group to which we wish to belong. We also use our EQ for self-understanding, to recognize the motivations that actually drive our behavior. Both IQ and EQ are what the author James Carse calls "finite games," games played *within the boundaries*.[4] But there is something not complete about this. Human beings don't always want to play by the rules or adapt to the situation. We are a cussed species. We often say, "I don't like this situation, it could be better, it could be different," and then we act to change it. When we do that, we are using our SQ.

SQ allows us to play an "infinite game." It allows us to *play with the boundaries*. It allows us to change the rules or to write new ones. It allows us to criticize the what-is from the point of view of what-might-be. It is the intelligence that allows us to imagine situations and possibilities that do not yet exist. SQ is a transformative intelligence that allows us to break old paradigms and to invent new ones. From its ability to recontextualize problems and situations and to see them from a wider point of view, SQ has the ability to dissolve old patterns and old ways of thinking. It also has the force to dissolve old motivations and move us on to higher ones. Thus, SQ provides a basis for a kind of meta-strategic thinking—strategic thinking that can stand back from and assess strategies themselves.

So far as present research can establish, our three intelligences act independently of each other. A person can be very high in IQ, but low in EQ or SQ, high in SQ but low in one of the other two, and so on. Erisychthon, the Greek timber merchant who brought a curse upon himself for felling a tree sacred to the gods, was probably very high in IQ. He was a successful businessman. We don't know much about Erisychthon's emotional intelligence, but it was his low SQ that brought about his self-destruction. He couldn't comprehend that one tree was special and of sacred significance because he had no sense of the sacred in the first place. It was as though he were color-blind, but his own blindness was to the meaning of things.

The Scientific Evidence for SQ

The hardware in the brain for making IQ and EQ possible has been known for some time. IQ is facilitated by a kind of brain wiring known as "serial wiring," where neural cells (neurons) are wired in a linear, point-to-point or one-on-one fashion, like a string of Christmas tree lights. This is the same kind of wiring found in PCs. EQ is facilitated by neural configurations known as "neural networks," where bundles containing approximately 100,000 neurons are wired in a messy fashion internally to each other. There are also neural network computers available today (parallel processors) that are used for recognizing patterns such as faces, tastes, fingerprints, and smells. Where IQ serial wiring is laid down by the brain's learning rules, EQ neural networks are formed by the associations we make in life between different things. A young child, for instance, associates mother with love, home with comfort, barking dogs with danger, fire with pain, and so on. Both serial wiring and neural networks are found all over the brain.

Scientific evidence for the existence of a third intelligence that uses values, meaning, and purpose first appeared toward the end of the 1990s. It had been known for some time that a need for meaning has played a crucial role in human evolution and human survival. The work of Harvard neuroscientist and anthropologist Terence Deacon had shown that it was a quest for meaning that first led to our species' need for language, and that the evolution of language in turn accounted for the rapid growth of the human forebrain.[5] And Viktor Frankl's work had demonstrated the psychological importance of meaning. But toward the end of the 1990s it was announced that neuroscientists had discovered a "God Spot" in the brain.[6]

The so-called God Spot is a mass of neural tissue located in the brain's temporal lobes, a region found just behind the temples. This neural mass is dedicated to making us ask fundamental questions of meaning about existence and to making us search for fundamental answers. It causes us to be idealistic and to search for ideal solutions to problems. The God Spot makes us aspire to higher things, to dream of better tomorrows. It is also active when we have spiritual experiences—a profound sense of love, a deep sense of peace, a sense of the unity of existence, profound beauty. In religious people, the God Spot is active when they feel they are in contact with the truths of their religion.

In the late 1990s, scientists discovered the God Spot by artificially stimulating the temporal lobe area with a magnetic probe. When so stimulated, one atheistic neuroscientist even claimed to have "seen God" in his laboratory. In similar experiments, research subjects were wired up with magnetic sensors at their temporal lobes and asked to think about what they found most sacred in life. Some thought of general things like peace, love, or unity, others of religious figures like Christ or the Buddha. But when the subjects did think about whatever was sacred to them, the magnetic sensors registered strong magnetic activity in the brain's temporal lobes.

The God Spot on its own cannot be the full basis of spiritual intelligence, because its activity is not always intelligent—that is, in any way apt to promote the quality of life. This same area of the brain is highly active in borderline schizophrenics and during manic episodes, and may indicate the person registering the high activity is seeing little green men in the kitchen sink rather than asking profound questions about the meaning of life. To produce intelligent spiritual experience, God Spot activity must be fully integrated with wider brain activity, and with IQ and EQ. How this is done was also discovered during the second half of the 1990s.

How the brain integrates and makes a whole of its experience had long been a mystery to science. How, for instance, when we are stimulated at every moment by thousands of perceptual data striking the trillions of neurons that make up the brain, is it possible for us to see the data as something like another person, a watch, or a tree? Why are we not all madly schizophrenic? This mystery was known as "the binding problem"—literally, how does the brain bind its experience together? The answer came only when new technology allowed the discovery of a wholly unexpected phenomenon.

In research pioneered by Wolf Singer,[7] it was discovered that neurons in the human brain vibrate in unison in response to particular stimuli. If you look at the face of a watch, for instance, one part of the brain vibrates in response to the roundness of the face, another part to the hands on the watch, still another part to the meaning of time, and so on through a whole range of features. But when you look at the watch, *all* those neurons in the brain that are responding do so by vibrating coherently, in unison. Uninvolved neurons do not vibrate at the same frequency. The vibrations, or oscillations, take place at 40 Hz—40 cycles per second. The same thing happens when you see a particular person or have a particular idea. The brain unifies its experience in each case by vibrating the relevant neurons in unison at approximately 40 Hz.

These 40 Hz neural oscillations move as a background wave all across the brain whenever human beings are conscious. They move in a carrier wave from the front of the skull to the back of the skull, and then get modified by different perceptual or cognitive experiences. Indeed, it is now known these 40 Hz oscillations *are* the neural basis for consciousness in the brain. They also work to unify all things that need to be unified for the brain to work as a whole unit. They unify all the brain's many expert systems (numeracy, language, sight, hearing, and all the rest), and they unify IQ and EQ with the SQ activities of the God Spot. They do so by searching out wider and deeper, more complex patterns of meaning within our disparate experience. These 40 Hz oscillations, combined with God Spot activity, are most likely the neural basis for the particular characteristics and qualities of our SQ. SQ itself enables us to become the fully intellectual, emotional, and spiritual beings that we might be.

Being something actually hardwired into our brains, both through the God Spot and through the 40 Hz activity, the search for and use of meaning (our SQ) is clearly a basic quality of our humanity. It is a natural potentiality of our brains, and lies at the heart of our ability to make sense of the world and other people. It also accounts for the sense of unity we have about ourselves—our sense of "I-ness," or of personal identity. This is one reason why we need to use SQ in organizations to get a deep sense of organizational identity, a sense of the personality and purpose of our organizations, a sense of what they are *about*.

A Field of Shared Meaning

Spiritual intelligence is different from both IQ and emotional intelligence. Lower animals have both of the latter in varying degrees. So far as we know, spiritual intelligence is our uniquely human ability to make moral choices and to embrace deeper meanings. It is the intelligence that defines our humanity. It would be natural, therefore, for us to wonder where it comes from and whether our access to it is in any way enhanced by a shared phenomenon such as culture. Are there features of SQ that enable an individual to raise the SQ of a culture or, looked at from the other direction, can a high-SQ culture raise the SQ of individuals? These questions are important to underpinning the central theme of this book—that a critical mass of individual leaders can indeed raise the SQ of a culture, which in turn can reach back and influence the levels of SQ in larger masses of people.

Materialistic scientists would not ask such questions. For them, everything in this world consists of material atoms. Brains consist of neurons made of atoms. Something like higher meaning or even consciousness itself is seen merely as an experienced or emergent by-product of neural processes. It makes no sense to ask where SQ, or consciousness itself, "comes from." It is just sufficient to say that we have these experiences because we have a God Spot in the temporal lobes and because our neurons oscillate at 40 Hz. As neuroscientist Francis Crick, who won the Nobel Prize for his work on DNA, puts this materialist position, "You, your joys and your sorrows, your memories and your ambitions, your sense of personal identity and free will, are in fact no more than the behaviour of a vast assembly of nerve cells and their associated molecules."[8] We just *think* we have minds!

I find the materialist position inadequate to explain my own experiences, those of thousands of people who have written about mind or soul from the world's great spiritual and philosophical traditions, both East and West, and the 50–70 percent of us who have experienced some "higher reality," "infinite mind" or "infinite realm" during "peak experiences" at some point in our lives.

I side more with those who argue that brains are the "hardware" and mind the "software" of our conscious mental experience. In this case mind, and especially the meanings and values accessed by spiritual intelligence, has a reality of its own (physical or otherwise) that needs brains to interact with this Newtonian, material world. The brain, following from this argument, is like a television set that enables us to pick up and process some of the patterns written on a wider, shared "mind-field," which would contain a field of shared meaning. A great deal of psychological evidence supports this view.

Over two thousand years ago Plato described a universal Realm of Ideas that individual minds tapped into to form our more limited and separate concepts. There was a universal Idea of Truth, of Goodness, of Beauty, and even universal Ideas of things like apples and chairs. Plato believed that individual human beings could communicate with each other, however imperfectly, and share a culture of ideas only because we shared our access to the universal Ideas.

In the twentieth century, the great Catholic philosopher Pierre Teilhard de Chardin proposed a similar idea with his suggestion of a *noosphere,* separate from the material biosphere. Again, Teilhard de Chardin's *noosphere* was a realm of shared concepts and meanings that formed a layer of an individual's conscious life.

A few years later, Carl Jung proposed his theory of the Collective Unconscious, a shared layer of our mental life that is peopled by archetypes, meanings, and large-scale, traumatic events. Jung believed that much of our dream life, and the universal themes that recur in myths from many diverse cultures, originate in this Collective Unconscious. He also felt that the Collective Unconscious underlay the countless experiences of telepathy between individuals and the synchronicity of apparently separate but co-meaningful events. Jung's views were similar to those that support the notion of a *zeitgeist*, or "spirit of the age."

In 1984, American psychologist and family therapist E. Bruce Taub-Bynum took the notion of the Collective Unconscious two important steps further. First, in his extensive work with families, he noted that members of family groups appear to share a "family unconscious."[9] He suggested this partly personal, partly shared domain of the unconscious accounted for the shared or similar dreams, lingering feelings and attitudes, collective assumptions, parenting styles, role assignments, and recurring behavior patterns (like addiction or abuse) that we find in family groups. Taub-Bynum argued that this family unconscious crossed generations, and features of it sometimes skipped generations.

Taub-Bynum's second important step was to describe this unconscious family matrix as a field that acts both within individual family members and also *between* family members. He proposed it was akin to, or perhaps even identical with, the electromagnetic, gravitational, or quantum fields that we find in physics. As he put it,

> The concept of fields of force or interactional levels borrowed from physics is helpful in understanding this family matrix. *A classical field in physics is a kind*

> of "tension" or "stress" which can exist in
> empty space in the absence of matter. It
> reveals itself by producing forces which act
> on any material objects that happen to lie
> in the space occupied by the field. Thus
> fields can account for action at a distance
> through empty space and explain how
> distant objects can act on one another. . . .
> Fields bring objects separated by space
> into relationship with one another.[10]

In fact, all these fields—electromagnetic, gravitational, and quantum—exist in and surround our bodies (including our brains). Various late-twentieth-century scientists have suggested that one or all of these fields may be implicated in our conscious life.[11]

Following Taub-Bynum's logic, I suggest these same shared unconscious fields are present among any group of people who live or work closely together. Each organization or institution will have its own, largely unconscious, field of shared meanings and emotions. Indeed, in our highly connected global society, there may be wider cultural or global fields of the shared unconscious. One tantalizing, ongoing experiment suggests precisely this.

Since 1977, a research group led by Dean Radin and centered at Princeton in the United States, has been conducting an ongoing test to see whether large-scale conscious events have any effect on electronic sensors located at different parts of the world. The research team have placed about fifty electronic random number generators (RNGs) on the globe's various continents. All are connected back to a central archive at Princeton. As these are random number generators, we would normally expect their fluctuations to be unconnected, and usually they are. But when large-scale events affecting whole masses of humanity happened, the generators' activity became correlated. There was a very significant correlation during the funeral of Diana, Princess of Wales, and another on September 11, 2001, when the Twin Towers were destroyed by terrorists. The odds against such correlations being coincidence are 10,000:1. The research team interprets these results as being evidence of both the existence of a worldwide field of meaning or consciousness and of the interaction of this field of meaning with matter (the RNGs).[12]

For the purpose of understanding human motives and how spiritual intelligence might shift them, it is enough to say that there most likely is a shared field of meaning and consciousness, whatever its underlying physical basis or lack of one. We are all immersed in it and interact with it. This allows us to see motivational states as "attractors" (points of focused energy) in this field (like the holes in the pinball machine), and SQ as some active principle of transformation within it. The questions now are, What qualities or processes of SQ act as motivational transformers? What are the *active, dynamic principles* of SQ? I turn to these in the next chapter. First, though, a postscript about Mats Lederhausen.

What Became of Mats

I began this chapter with the quandary Mats brought to me, "What should I do?" Mats (and the business world) were lucky. What Mats wound up doing was to write a letter to Jack Greenburg, CEO of McDonald's, expressing his concerns. To his surprise, he was invited to Chicago for a chat and got the promotion he had thought unlikely. Now holding the title of Vice President Strategy and responsible for "leveraging change," Mats says he has been hired to be "a corporate pain in the ass." He spends much of his time speaking to McDonald's and other business executives in promotion of what he feels are good causes. At McDonald's itself, his tenure has been associated with the battle against genetically modified organisms, a campaign for larger chicken cages, and partnership with Conservation International to restore the globe's damaged ecosystems and to see how McDonald's can contribute toward sustainable agriculture. He is also one of the Davos World Economic Forum's Global Leaders of Tomorrow, which gives him a worldwide platform from which to nag. His high SQ, particularly his desire to fight for his vision and values, has led to a shift in his work motivation from -3, *craving* (working just for money) to at least $+3$, *power-within*. More accurately, I would place him at $+6$, *higher service*—one of the knights I discuss in Chapter Ten. "For the time being," he says, "I feel I am in the right place, doing the right thing."

The Twelve Principles
of Transformation

*Being new, nameless, hard to
understand, we premature births
of an as yet unproven future, we
need for a new goal also a new
means.*

—Nietzsche, *Ecce Homo*

Expanding spiritual capital is my goal in this book,
but it is a goal unlike any before. It requires that
we act from our higher, sometimes our highest,
motivations. It means that we transform ourselves as
human beings. To achieve this new goal, we need some
new *means*. For that we must look to the principles of
transformation available to spiritual intelligence.

As noted, a human being's IQ is pretty well steady
throughout life, barring brain illness or damage. But EQ,
or emotional intelligence, can be learned, nurtured, and
improved. And all human beings are born with a potential

for high SQ. Most children have a high potential for it. But our spiritually dumb culture and educational system, and our often spiritually deadening work patterns and pressures, reduce our capacity to practice our SQ. Like EQ, SQ must be nurtured. It can be relearned, and it can be improved. To do so, we must look for those qualities of a person's being and behavior that signify the presence of SQ at work. Finding and exploring these qualities also helps us understand SQ itself. But this requires that we ask what kind of *systems* or *organizations* we human beings are, and what kind of system is operating in the human brain when SQ is in use. To know a thing's qualities, we must know that thing itself.

At the purely simple scientific level, of course, human beings are biological systems, or living systems. But science today understands that living systems are very special systems, with unique qualities that distinguish them from most nonliving systems. So the search for the qualities of full human intelligence must slip sideways for a moment into this new science—into the realms of complexity theory and the complex adaptive systems that it describes.

In the 1960s, science moved away from its obsession with the simple to a celebration of the complex. Newtonian scientific theory describes systems that are simple. Such systems are linear, predictable, controllable, isolated, and consist of separate working parts into which the system can be broken down for analysis. The whole is just the sum of its parts. Newtonian systems models have been, and in many cases still are, applied to human systems like the market or business organizations. Without realizing it, most companies are still using simple Newtonian business models.

In addition to simple Newtonian systems, two other kinds of classic systems have come to be understood:

"complex systems" and "simple adaptive systems." Unlike a simple system, a complex system has many parts, and these interact. To understand the system, it's essential to understand these interactions—like the many parts that go to make up an automobile and the way their interaction gives rise to motion. Such mechanical complex systems are nonadaptive—they do not learn, do not evolve. The individual component parts of the systems do not alter through their interaction with each other or with the environment. Unfortunately, most "systems thinking" in the corporate world is modeled on these kinds of nonadaptive systems. That is why the usual brand of systems thinking has not been able to deliver deep transformation.

By contrast with mechanical systems, whether simple or complex, a simple adaptive system—though existing in isolation and having very few parts—can adapt, or evolve. Darwin's model of genetic mutation described such a system, where a single gene sometimes undergoes a random mutation. The environment in which the gene is located is at first unaffected, but the gene itself, and so the whole organism, is altered.

With the rise of complexity science some forty years ago, it became clear that living systems can follow a very different kind of evolutionary pattern. In looking more closely at how life operates in its environment, complexity biologists discovered a further kind of system known as a "complex adaptive system." These systems have many interacting parts and are in constant creative dialogue with their environment. They live at the edge of chaos. When the environment presents the system with a crisis, the whole mega-system (organism plus environment) *and* the elements within it "co-evolve."

These complex adaptive systems are nonlinear. They are unpredictable; attempts to control them are destructive, and they cannot be broken down into separate, more simple parts. A living system poised at the edge of chaos has to be seen as a whole, and that whole is greater than the sum of its parts. Where Newtonian simple systems are designed by blueprint or according to Newton's three laws of motion, complex adaptive systems emerge through self-organization. Where Newtonian systems are the same in all conditions, never subject to any internal change, complex adaptive systems creatively explore their own futures as they adapt to and evolve within an environment to which they are internally sensitive. And where Newtonian simple systems are stable, complex systems can be radically unstable, their instability allowing them to thrive at the edge of chaos.

The edge of chaos itself represents a new, third kind of order in the universe. Any system, if not disturbed, will settle into a small number of its possible states, which are stable. These stable states in any field are called *attractors*. (Our motives are attractors in a field of meaning.) If the system is challenged or disturbed too much, it can spin off into chaos, where there is no discernable or predictable order. But when complex adaptive systems are presented with a crisis, they are drawn to the edge of chaos. This is a point between order and disorder. The elements of the system are just ordered enough to be in a number of semistable states, but these are easily upset by the smallest perturbation. When this happens, the system searches in every direction for new attractors to settle into, creating new order and new information in the process. The principles of transformation that the system uses to find its new state are the same as those we will need to shift our motives from old attractors to new ones.

All living things have the capacity to be such systems, from the one-celled amoeba to ourselves, our organizations, and our culture. We are complex adaptive systems poised at the edge of chaos. In human beings, our immune systems are poised at the edge of chaos, as are our heartbeats, much of our brain activity, and certainly our mental activity when we are thinking creatively. SQ is also a complex adaptive intelligence poised at the edge of chaos. That is why it can make and break existing paradigms and dissolve fixed patterns of thought or behavior. It composes its self-organizing patterns of meaning as these emerge in a creative dialogue between our minds and their environment. The brain's many interactive complex adaptive systems interact with the field of meaning.

SQ is needed for times of crisis, when our habitual attitudes fail us, and something new and creative is needed. But in more familiar situations, far from chaos, IQ and EQ are often sufficient, and use much less energy. When SQ must come into play, we're apt to be reminded of the old Chinese curse, "May you live in interesting times!"

SQ is a recently discovered intelligence, and there has as yet been little clinical research on the human qualities with which it can be associated. But as SQ functions as a complex adaptive system in the mind, the better-researched and more clearly understood qualities of these systems seem an obvious first place to look for identifying qualities of SQ itself. In looking to these biological systems as models or forerunners of SQ qualities, however, it's essential to bear in mind that SQ is a *conscious* complex adaptive system, and thus its qualities will have a uniquely conscious expression.

Complex adaptive systems have ten distinctive characteristics that give them their uniquely creative mode of operating in the world. Since these are the qualities that give rise to the system's creative evolution, they can be seen as the principles of transformation within the system. "Mind" itself, our consciousness and its structured contents, is itself a complex adaptive system that emerges when brain meets the field of meaning. Thus these principles of transformation are also principles of transformation (learning, evolution) within consciousness. They are the transformative principles (in part) that give SQ its paradigm-breaking and paradigm-making abilities. And they are the transformative principles that will underlie any attempt to shift human motives, and therefore behavior. These are the ten principles:

- *Self-organizing.* These systems have a deep order sleeping within, but this order is a potentiality that then takes on whatever form it will adopt as the system self-organizes in dialogue with the environment.
- *Bounded instability.* These systems exist only at the edge of chaos, in a zone of instability that falls just between order and chaos. They are described as being "far from equilibrium." If they were wholly unstable, they would disintegrate into chaos. If they were wholly ordered, they would be inflexible and nonadaptive.
- *Emergent.* These systems are larger than the sum of their parts. The whole has qualities and properties that the individual parts don't possess, and this whole emerges only as the system adapts to and evolves within its environment.
- *Holistic.* These systems have no internal boundaries, no recognizably separate parts. Each part is entangled with and impinges upon every other part. The parts are internally defined through their relationship to each other and to the environment.

- *Adaptive.* These systems not only learn as they go, they create themselves as they act to explore their own futures. This adaptation is always in mutually self-creative dialogue with an environment to which they are internally sensitive.

- *Evolutionary mutations.* Mutations play a creative role in the final emergent structure of these systems' future.

- *Destroyed by outside control.* The delicately poised internal order and balance of these systems is destroyed if we try to impose control from the outside. Their own self-organization collapses and they revert to being simple or complex Newtonian systems.

- *Exploratory.* These systems are constantly exploring their own possible futures and creating themselves as they go.

- *Recontextualizing.* These systems reframe their own inner development as they recontextualize (relearn) the boundaries and qualities of their environment.

- *Order out of chaos.* These systems create order out of chaos; they have "negative entropy." They bring new form into an unformed or unstructured arena.

From these properties of complex adaptive systems, I can draw ten qualities of a spiritually intelligent complex adaptive system (a human being!), bearing in mind the added factor of consciousness and the effect that a conscious expression would have on the quality. I have also added two additional qualities of SQ derived simply from characteristics identified by the vast spiritual literature of the ages. Thus though nonhuman complex adaptive systems have ten defining qualities, I see a total of *twelve* qualities definitive of a human being with spiritual intelligence. These are the twelve criteria for a person or an organization high in SQ, and the twelve principles of transformation that allow SQ to dissolve old motives and create new ones:

- *Self-awareness.* To know what I believe in and value and what deeply motivates me. Awareness of my deepest life's purposes.
- *Spontaneity.* To live in and be responsive to the moment and all that it contains.
- *Being vision and value led.* Acting from principles and deep beliefs, and living life accordingly.
- *Holism* (a sense of the system, or of connectivity). Ability to see larger patterns, relationships, connections. A strong sense of belonging.
- *Compassion.* Quality of "feeling-with" and deep empathy. Ground-work for *universal sympathy.*
- *Celebration of diversity.* Valuing other people and unfamiliar situations for their differences, not despite them.
- *Field independence.* To be able to stand against the crowd and maintain my own convictions.
- *Tendency to ask fundamental why? questions.* Need to understand things, to get to the bottom of them. Basis for criticizing the given.
- *Ability to reframe.* Stand back from the problem or situation and look for the bigger picture, the wider context.
- *Positive use of adversity.* Ability to own and learn from mistakes, to see problems as opportunities. Resilience.
- *Humility.* Sense of being a player in a larger drama, sense of my true place in world. Basis for self-criticism and critical judgment.

- *Sense of vocation.* Being "called" to serve something larger than myself. Gratitude toward those who have helped me, and a wish to give something back. Basis for the "servant leader."

There is little point in saying just a bit more about these qualities here. They are too important for that. In the cultivation and practice of these qualities and transformation processes lies our ability to use our whole brains, our ability to know and practice our deepest meanings and purposes, our ability to bring transformation to our lives and to the situations in which we operate, and our ability to think at the edge of chaos. They allow us to know deeply and to recontextualize our experience. They allow us to make contact with our own souls and to place ourselves at the heart of the deepest possible human being. They are the active principles

TABLE 6.1 Common Features of Complex Adaptive Systems and Spiritual Intelligence

Complex Adaptive Systems	Spiritual Intelligence
Self-organization	Self-awareness
Bounded instability	Spontaneity
Emergent	Vision and value led
Holistic	Holistic
In dialogue with environment	Compassion (feeling-with)
Evolutionary mutations	Celebration of diversity
Outside control destructive	Field-independent
Exploratory	Asking why?
Recontexualize environment	Reframe
Order out of chaos	Positive use of adversity
	Humility
	Sense of vocation

with which we can build spiritual capital. And these twelve qualities are also the basis for a wider understanding of strategic planning in organizations and a sound basis for extending our usual notion of the bottom line. Because of all this, I will explore each quality at some length in the next chapter.

Applying the Principles of Transformation

This chapter outlines in some detail the defining characteristics of each of the twelve transformative processes of SQ. That will put me in a good position then to link them with the Scale of Motivations and the dynamics of permanent cultural shift.

Self-Awareness

Chris Miller, CEO of Anglian Water in the United Kingdom, says, "If you really want to be a leader, the first thing you have to understand is yourself." Two millennia earlier, Jesus promised his disciples, "If you know who you are, you will become as I am." Yet knowing who we are is perhaps the last thing we know.

We live in a very self-obsessed culture, but we have very little self-awareness. Neither in our personal lives nor in our organizations do we have many habits or structures for reflection. We take little or no time for catching up with ourselves, for looking inward. We don't even have any recent tradition for showing us what we might look inward *for,* or why. Our focus is outward, on events and problems in the world, with the consequence that we lose ourselves and all that is to be gained from self-knowledge.

In many parts of the East where Hinduism and Buddhism are widely practiced, people begin their day with this meditation or prayer:

> Who is it that is acting?
> Who is it that is willing?
> Who is it that is thinking?
> Who am I?

These questions take us directly to the deepest and most spiritual level of self-awareness—an awareness that we have a "deep self" in the first place, a personal reality that lies beneath and acts through our daily actions and thoughts. This primary level of self-awareness enables us to escape the narrow restrictions imposed by our mere egos. The questions take us to the center of our awareness and freedom and empower us to act from our highest motives.

The awareness that I, or the organization of which I am a part, has a deep center in the first place, and that I need to be in contact with it and to act through it, confers meaning and authenticity on my projects and actions. It is exhilarating to know that I have an inner compass and that I can be led by its sense of direction. This is one crucial meaning of integrity—to act in accord with my inner compass. To have self-awareness at this level is to know what I believe in, what I value, and what deeply motivates me. It is to know what I live for and, perhaps, even what I would die for. It is also having the courage to know when I am betraying these things.

Because deep self-awareness puts us (and our organizations) in touch with our deepest center, it allows us to create or re-create ourselves continuously. It puts us in touch with a font of infinite potentiality. It also enables us to hear the call of the deep self, the voice of conscience and responsibility. It gives us a sense of focus and often confers a deep sense of peace.

Daniel Goleman has argued that self-awareness is the keystone of emotional intelligence. If I don't know what or how I feel, emotions will control me and my reactions. "An inability to notice my true feelings," he warns, "leaves me at their mercy." Knowing our deepest values and purposes is the keystone of our spiritual intelligence and allows us to raise and control our motivations.[1]

Opposites: Without deep self-awareness, we are superficial and ego-bound, at the mercy of whim, wild emotion, and our lowest motivations. We are blind and insensitive to our inner lives and easily distracted by the activities and goals of daily life. We blunder through our own and others' lives leaving a trail of unwanted consequences.

Common Distortions: In our Western culture, "self-awareness" is often just self-obsession, too much "me, me, me." There is a tendency to get sidetracked by fads and techniques that feed the ego—diets, exercise, New Age practices—and to get lost in or obsessed with them, missing the whole point of genuine self-discovery.

How to Nurture: A practice of daily meditation or reflection, participation in genuine dialogue, being willing to enter my discomfort zone to face unpleasant truths about myself, finding space and time during the day to "hear" myself, having a quiet, meditative or personal space to which I can occasionally retreat (what would such a space look like for you?), reviewing the events of the day and my responses to them. When was I most authentic (inauthentic)?

Self-Awareness Check
- Do you have much sense of an inner life?
- At the end of the day, do you reflect on the day's events and experiences?
- Do you have any sense of a deeper presence within you?
- Are you comfortable with silence?
- Can you confront uncomfortable truths about yourself?

Spontaneity

During one of the final rounds of the men's Wimbledon Tennis Tournament two or three years ago, there were some amazing acrobatics. One of the players—Andre Agassi, I believe, tripped during a volley and fell forward onto his chest. Nonetheless, he kept his head and right arm up and returned the ball just across the net. Then, standing up and with a second volley coming right toward him, Agassi lost his balance again and began to fall backward. This time he returned the volley in the midst of his backward fall and managed to win the point.

Agassi's winning shots were a combination of fierce inner discipline combined with the most radical spontaneity. Though off his balance both times, he was still instantly responsive to the position and momentum of the ball. He was in what sports psychologists call "the zone." This kind of being in the zone is our closest Western equivalent to the disciplined spontaneity practiced by the martial artist. It is action or response that comes from beyond the ego, that issues from the "deep self." When in it, we are connected to our personal center, and hence to our inner power.

The word *spontaneity* comes from the same Latin root as the words *response* and *responsibility*. To be deeply spontaneous is to be deeply responsive to the moment, and then willing and able to take responsibility for it. It means greeting each moment, each person, each situation with the freshness of a child, without all the baggage of past conditioning, habit, prejudice, fear, needing to seize control, or being unnecessarily polite. It means having the courage to put myself in the moment. Deep spontaneity is, therefore, the necessary precondition for playfulness, improvisation, trial-and-error learning, and creativity. This is particularly true for mental spontaneity.

Mental spontaneity is the condition of being "in the zone" with our thinking. Too often we take refuge in what we already know, what we have already learned, in conditioned habits of thought. We get trapped in our minds' own personal paradigms—dogmas, prejudices, ideologies to which we subscribe, abstractions and models, assumptions we hold, or simply thinking that feels comfortable and familiar. Mental spontaneity, like so many of the processes that distinguish SQ, often requires that we be willing to enter our discomfort zone. This can bring us face to face with fear.

Fear is usually the greatest barrier to achieving spontaneity. Fear of ridicule, fear of judgment or punishment, and fear of showing our own vulnerability. To be spontaneous, I must have the courage to suspend my defenses and to own both my vulnerability and my authenticity. These put me in touch with the spiritual dimension of spontaneity—a radical openness to life's possibilities and an existential readiness to become the person who I really am. Both are frequently accompanied by a sense of deep joy or even ecstasy. Both require a deep trust in life, a deep trust in myself, and a trust that I have a deep inner authority or inner compass that guides me.

Opposites: The opposites of spontaneity are practicing too much control, being too rigid, lacking self-confidence (and confidence in life), being "constipated." Habit and too high a regard for tradition are often the enemies of spontaneity, as is too high a regard for authority—deep spontaneity is often of necessity deeply subversive. The freshness of the child is inseparable from the subversiveness of the child.

Common Distortions: True spontaneity is not impulsiveness or merely acting on a whim of the moment. Both are distortions of a very demanding and highly disciplined reality. Someone who is merely impulsive or unthinking is usually insensitive to or unresponsive to the deep currents of another person or of a situation. True spontaneity is the freshness of the child honed by the wisdom, strength, and experience of the adult.

How to Nurture: Nurturing spontaneity in its deepest sense probably requires a discipline like daily meditation. To be deeply spontaneous, we have to be deeply aware—of ourselves, of others, of situations, and of their respective potentials. We also need to expose ourselves to unfamiliar situations and people and note our responses. Review each day at the end, asking yourself, What missed opportunities did it contain? Why did I not speak my mind? Why did I not show my true emotions? Why did I not let myself go with enthusiasm or passion? What stopped me? Do I believe in myself?

Spontaneity Check
- Do you follow your gut instincts, even if it means taking risks?
- Do you allow yourself to be open and vulnerable with others?

- Do you enjoy talking to and playing with young children?
- Do you ever feel an ecstatic sense that the whole of reality or existence is present for you now, "in this moment"?
- Do you feel that an underlying sense of direction or inner compass guides you?

Vision and Value Led

In August 1963, I was among a crowd of some 100,000 people gathered before the Lincoln Memorial on the Mall in Washington, D.C. We had prepared for this event all summer, and a great excitement filled the crowd. But none of us could have imagined or foreseen the electrifying wave of inspirational energy that swept through us as Martin Luther King Jr. almost sang out the ringing phrases of his now famous "I Have a Dream" speech. His words, their passion and the vision they offered, galvanized us, fired our motivations, and transformed the social and political landscape of our country. That is what real visions do.

Dr. King's words reached beyond the given realities of American race relations and painted the picture of a new, more just and loving society scarcely imagined by the American people at that time. He palpably ached in the whole of his being for the not-yet-born, and that ache carried in his voice as an inspirational longing. This, too, is a vital feature of great visions. They reach deep into a well of human potentiality and present us with the not-yet-born. They make us dream, They make us long. They motivate us. It was with a similarly powerful vision that Mahatma Gandhi led India to independence and Nelson Mandela ended apartheid in South Africa. And that same visionary spirit lay behind Merck

Pharmaceutical's gift of a cure for river blindness to the Third World, behind Henry Ford's vision of bringing transport to the common man, and Coca-Cola's construction of health clinics throughout rural China and Southeast Asia.

Visions give rise to new realities through raising human motivations. But visions themselves are based on deep values. The founder of Merck valued health and bringing health to people, Martin Luther King Jr. valued equality and human dignity. Values are like quanta of energy. They make things happen. Our deepest values define us as the human beings that we are and lay the foundations for the kinds of organizations and societies that will bring out the best of human potential. If we want to shift human and corporate motivation beyond its currently low level on the Scale of Motivations, we can do so only through a healthy dose of the idealism that flows from serving fundamental values.

Nearly all companies these days talk about the values they claim to hold. Many print them on little cards for employees to carry round in their wallets. How do these facile attempts to appear value-driven differ from serving really fundamental values? They differ in both the spirit and the content of really living by values. For fundamental values, Plato's big three—Goodness, Truth, and Beauty—are quite a good start. Others are life, liberty, and the pursuit of happiness, or fidelity, respect, and service.

In Table 7.1 I have gathered a short list of some fundamental values. Many others could be added. All fall into one or more of three categories: personal values (relating to my own life—my friends, my family, my interests); interpersonal values (things that define my group and the relations between members of that group—like loyalty, and trust); and transpersonal values (values

TABLE 7.1 An Array of Values

Excellence	Honesty	Mercy	Friendship	Health
Humility	Order	Compassion	Austerity	Respect for property
Service	Liberty	Respect	Awareness	Loyalty
Gratitude	Harmony	Life	Regard for future generations	Respect for ancestors
Truth	Equality	Fidelity	Altruism	
Beauty	Stewardship	Tolerance	Politeness	
Balance	Modesty	Forgiveness	Privacy	
Public good	Happiness	Love	Obedience	
Respect for elders	Commitment	Protection of children	Education	
Saving face	Justice	Maintenance of family	Wisdom	

that transcend my own person and group, values I consider to be universal values, like the sanctity of life, pro-
tecting the world for future generations, or justice). The
great German philosopher Immanuel Kant had a moral
imperative that was the basis for his system of values:
"Always act in such a way that it would be all right if
everyone acted that way." This may well be a good criterion for all values, but it certainly applies to transpersonal values. It would be very creative if it could apply to
corporate values.

Opposites: To be vision and value led is to be idealistic,
unselfish, and dedicated. Thus the opposites are to be
cynical or overly pragmatic, self-serving, and oppor-
tunistic. Other opposites are to be very materialist, lazy,
or undisciplined. Realpolitik is an excuse for jettisoning
values for the sake of selfish or short-term gain. Where a
value-driven person or organization reaches beyond the
given and raises the game, cynicism uses the given as an
excuse ("Everybody does it.")—and usually lowers the
game.

Common Distortions: A visionary can be so caught up in
a vision as to lose touch with reality, or with the negative possibilities of a vision. This can lead to closed-
mindedness, fanaticism, a dictatorial leadership style,
blinkered vision, or an insensitivity to pragmatic reality
and daily necessities ("a mere dreamer"). Adolf Hitler
was a great visionary, but he did not serve fundamental
human values.

How to Nurture: Give vent to our highest aspirations,
think about an opportunity or a situation: How could it
be? Perhaps make a resolution each week to raise the
game at work or in my personal life—and arrange for a

small reward or punishment. Review my values and goals. Are they really what I live for? Am I living true to them? In an organization, ask if this organization is really about something worthwhile? If not, what changes would make it so? What changes would inspire people and raise their motivations?

Vision and Values Check
- Are you motivated by ideals like helping others or serving some higher cause?
- Do you live by your ideals?
- Do you feel called upon "to go that extra mile" to bring excellence to whatever you do?
- Do you feel inspired by great leaders or public figures, historical or contemporary?
- Do you reflect on questions like the meaning of life, the purpose of your life, the meaning behind your work or relationships?

Holism

At Blue Circle Cement they had a problem with profit margins. Delivery costs were running too high and the company had pretty much decided to cut back on trips, and thus on drivers. The company had earlier adopted a policy of open dialogue and full consultation with employees, so a meeting was called to discuss the problem and to announce job cuts. A tanker driver named Bill spoke up at this meeting.

"The problem isn't the number of trips and drivers," Bill said emphatically. "It's the size of the gas tanks." A bemused CEO asked Bill to explain his thinking. Bill then pointed out that Blue Circle's gas tanks were designed for long-distance journeys of three hundred to four hundred miles, whereas the average journey per delivery was only eighty miles. "All that weight could be used for carrying cement," he said, and then added, "You should also look at the weight of our metal hoses." When technical experts followed through on these observations, they discovered that General Motors could supply trucks with smaller tanks at less cost, and that the heavy metal hoses could be replaced with light plastic ones. When these changes were made, productivity rose by 500 percent in the first six months without job cuts.

Blue Circle's action was holistic to begin with because it had in place a system of consultation that enabled a simple driver to speak up and be taken seriously by the bosses. And that driver's thinking was holistic because he looked at the productivity problem as a *full system* problem. He considered the interplay and connectedness of individual factors bearing on delivery costs, and thus brought a fresh perspective to the problem.

Holism in science is a defining quality of both quantum and complex adaptive self-organizing systems. It is an internal holism in that the relationship of the different parts of the system helps to define not just the system itself but even to give final form to the parts themselves. In physical holism, *it is the relationship between things that defines their reality.* You can't break a holistic system down into its separate parts without losing something vital of both those parts and of the system they comprise. You can't isolate the individual factors within the system. This is one of the qualities that made twentieth-century science revolutionary and paradigm breaking.

Holism is also a defining quality of and process within using SQ. It is an ability to see larger patterns and relationships, an ability to see the internally functioning connections between things, the overlaps and influences. It is an ability to look at a problem from every angle and to see that every question has at least two sides, and usually more. It is also a perception that a deeper common reality underlies most differences. Seeing the holistic nature of a problem also taps into the deeper potentiality within the situation from which it arises. (Most situations include possibilities analogous to Blue Circle's use of smaller gas tanks and lighter hoses instead of cutting back on the workforce.) At its most "spiritual" level, holism gives us the ability to see the infinite within the finite. And it gives us access to the deeper currents and patterns of a problem or situation. It taps us into possibilities.

Holistic people rely heavily on intuition, which is itself simply the initial and pre-logical perception of patterns, relationships, and coherences. A holistic thinker is reflective and broad-minded, living life on a bigger stage. Such people are sensitive to the inner workings of groups or situations. They take responsibility for their part within the whole and are always aware of how that whole affects them and others. Such people are needed to address, for example, the overwhelming problems issuing from human actions affecting the environment, and to appreciate that the environment human beings create impinges upon our own well-being. The same is true of perceiving the complex interrelationships and patterns within a globalized economy, the social, political, and spiritual issues that bear on and create economic reality.

Traditionally, organizations have been described as machines, or as collections of individuals (or at best, collections of teams) united by rules, practices, and a "culture." But this is bitty and piecy. The holistic aspect of SQ enables those parts or individuals to become a system and allows, literally, our organizations to become complex, self-organizing adaptive systems, with all the creativity that implies. It breathes life into a system from below, from the deep well of potentiality latent within the system.

In my view, the real glue or holistic underpinning of a society or an organization (or even of an individual) is its vision and deep values, its sense of being about something meaningful. This is the driving force that binds together and motivates any human complex system and ensures its function. An organization works when it is aware, at least unconsciously, of this driving vision and values and is true to them. When it is not, it is bound to be dysfunctional. Preoccupation with the bottom line does not integrate or motivate at this level.

Opposites: The opposite of holism is atomism—a tendency to see life, work, and problems as a collection of separate parts. To be atomistic is to be fragmented, to let thoughts or actions function in isolation, without regard or sensitivity to the whole or to the bigger picture. Atomistic people get lost in the details, they "can't see the forest for the trees." Such people are often partisan or parochial, their thinking limited to local or immediate conditions and blinkered by the immediate. The prevalence of short-term thinking in business and politics is symptomatic of atomism.

Common Distortions: Holism can be taken too far as well. At the extreme, you risk getting lost in the big picture and thus becoming too insensitive to the importance of detail, becoming undiscriminating or irresponsible. ("It's all too much for me.")

How to Nurture: Look for a unifying or emerging theme running through a course of events. Look for the wider context within which a problem has arisen. Follow through a chain of causal connections leading to this moment or concrete situation, and the chain of consequences likely to follow from the action you take in response. Take an actual event or action of some significance and follow through the steps that led up to it and those things that followed from it. How far back or forward can you trace the radiating lines of causality?

Holism Check
- Do you tend to look for relationships between apparently different things?
- Do you look for a wider context into which you can put problems or events?
- Do you have a sense that events or problems that come to your attention are interconnected?
- Do you have experiences of anticipating or knowing the unspoken thoughts of others, or sense a flow of energy coming from other people?
- Do you ever have a sense of everything being permeated by infinite love, infinite clarity or infinite presence?

Compassion

A Dutch investment banker whom I shall call "Geert" wrote to me with a request very similar to that of Mats Lederhausen of McDonald's. Like Mats, Geert was at the top of his career, the senior investment analyst for one of Holland's big banks. And like Mats, he wasn't happy. "I just spend all my time making money for myself and for my bank," he complained when we met. "There's a whole troubled world out there, and I feel I just have to do something about it." What Geert wanted from me was a little moral support for a decision he had already taken. A young man in his mid-thirties, he had decided to leave investment banking to set up a global ethical investment fund. Besides channeling his fund's money into ethical businesses, he intended to set aside 10 percent of all profits for the development of clean energy in the Third World.

In the Latin, *compassion* literally means "feeling with." A quality of deep empathy, compassion is not just knowing the feelings of others but feeling their feelings. It is knowing what it is like to walk in my neighbor's shoes, and perhaps wanting to help the journey that my neighbor makes less painful, less needy—for my neighbor's sake. Hence it is an active feeling-with, a willingness—no, almost a compulsion—to get involved. Compassion requires that I feel the common humanity of my neighbors even if their views are alien to or opposite to my own, feeling-with them at a deep level even if I have to kill or destroy them because they are my "enemy" and threaten me. We are often able, through compassion, to draw out the potentiality for good from within even the very bad. This is the nurturing aspect of the quality.

All psychological evidence shows that we are more likely to be compassionate toward or cooperative with someone from our own family or group than toward members of other groups. This is no longer good enough, given the global links that cause us to impinge upon one another even as strangers. A part of the paradigm shift to spiritual capital entails a paradigm shift about the so-called otherness of others. Can I call any person a stranger? Albert Einstein said that true compassion was compassion for the whole of existence, for every last speck of dust within it. Both quantum physics and the qualities of the universal field of meaning within which we all participate tell us that we are all pieces of each other, or at the very least all individual expressions of the same underlying reality. I am my brother's keeper because I am my brother.

True compassion requires the courage to be vulnerable and to own my vulnerability. My compassion for another is usually evoked by that other's vulnerability, but a healthy realization of "There but for the grace of God go I" prevents compassion from descending to mere pity. It acknowledges that today especially we all have a shared vulnerability. An honest awareness that now we are all in this together can lead to a very pressing sense of feeling-with the plight of others.

The word *passion* is also hidden within compassion. If I feel-with someone or something, it can fill me with a passionate intensity within, it can stir me. Hence again, stirring me to become involved, active. That is why it is associated with one of the highest of our motivations, *higher service.*

Opposites: A compassionate person is both sensitive and responsive. To feel no compassion is usually linked with insensitivity, cruelty, indifference, unresponsiveness, or cynicism. A person whose driving motives are self-interest or self-assertion is unlikely to feel much compassion for others.

Common Distortions: Sentimentality. To be pitying (which is a form of contempt) or bossy and interfering. To impose what I think best upon the other. To get carried away with my own enthusiasm and lose perspective.

How to Nurture: Become more honest about my own vulnerabilities. Be more aware of the consequences of my actions or feelings. Think, How would I feel if these were directed toward me? Do something regularly and gladly for others. Notice the things for which I am grateful and imagine being deprived of them.

Compassion Check
- Do you feel the feelings of others? Their pain? Their joy?
- Have you ever felt a universal sense of gentleness or nurturing love?
- Would you agree with the statement, "I am my brother's keeper because my brother is myself"?
- Have you ever felt a sense of reverence or awe for all of existence?
- Can you empathize with the pain, suffering, or anger of people who radically disagree with you, or who may even be a threat to you?

Celebrate Diversity

On a lecture tour of Finland I noticed and commented on the homogeneity of Finnish culture. "That is exactly our big problem," responded an executive from Nokia. "We are too alike. We all come from the same kind of schools, we went to the same few universities, and we all think alike. We lack the enrichment of diversity." In our more diverse Western nations and economies, with their now-common "diversity initiatives," *diversity* too often means having an acceptable number of people from ethnic backgrounds on the payroll and a token woman on the board of directors.

A full appreciation of real diversity and its benefits is difficult for Western people and organizations. For more than two thousand years, ever since Moses came down from Sinai with his Tablets of the Law, ours has been a culture of the One God, the one truth, the one way. This thinking runs through all Western religions, appears again in Newtonian science (absolute space, absolute time, universal laws of nature), and is even built into our logic: either/or rather than both/and. This gives Westerners a negative view of conflict and difference. We see conflict as something to be "resolved," usually through the defeat of any opponents. At best we tolerate difference, allowing it to coexist despite our disagreement or discomfort.

By contrast, complex adaptive systems in nature thrive on diversity. That bit of grit in the oyster becomes a pearl.

Genuine diversity means loving or at least highly valuing other people and conflicting opinions for their differences rather than despite those differences. It means seeing difference as opportunity. This requires, for Westerners, making the quantum leap of recognizing that truth is multifaceted, perhaps infinite, and that there is no "one best way." (Einstein's physics assumes as many valid points of view on space/time as there are observers; quantum physics makes the ground of all reality a field of infinite potentiality—the quantum vacuum.) A celebration of diversity recognizes that the best approximation to understanding a problem or evolving a strategy is to capture as many points of view on it as possible. This requires a recognition that what brings discomfort or challenges assumptions is often the best teacher.

A full celebration of diversity means almost thanking God for the other's difference, because that difference enriches my own reality and opportunities. This allows me to respect a point of view (a religion, a belief, an argument) as valid and thus worth consideration, even though it is different from mine. And this of course requires that

I be somewhat humble about the importance of my own opinion. All these qualities require that I (or my organization) be deeply secure enough in myself to question myself and possibly all that I hold sacred. For this I must cultivate a deep trust that truth will emerge from conflict, or from a situation's self-organizing potential, and must give up the need for total control.

A rich diversity underlies each one of us as individuals (and usually as organizations). Learning to appreciate it in others can help me learn to accept the rich chorus of my own many inner voices. This leaves me more open to intuition and hunches, more broad-minded and more open to life's or a situation's different possibilities. It makes me more flexible, more self-questioning, thoughtful, open to learning, and willing to grow.

There is a rich lesson to be learned about diversity from its role in natural complex adaptive systems. In science, homogeneous systems are very stable but hence slow to adapt. If an organization's dominant culture is too strong, it can share this flaw. By contrast, too much diversity or dissent in a system just tears it apart. Systems poised at the edge of chaos hold homogeneity and diversity in a critical balance. We might use the metaphor of "Her Majesty's Loyal Opposition" to illustrate the necessity of loyal dissent within a company culture.

Opposites: A person who cannot celebrate diversity sees only one way forward and tells everyone else, "It's my way or the highway." This leads to a dictatorial leadership style and narrow, exclusive attitudes. Such people are often narrow-minded, even arrogant, prejudiced, and insular. They are usually deeply insecure and in extremes can even become paranoid.

Common Distortions: Too much appreciation of diversity can leave me superficial, not being able to claim or relate to any point of view as my own. It can leave me vacillating, undiscriminating, and fearful of taking a stand. This in turn makes any commitment difficult.

How to Nurture: Participation in a dialogue mode of conversation with different others is essential. Try taking another's different point of view and really living it. See how it feels to wear the other's mind-set. Travel and expose myself to different cultures—within or outside my own country or organization—and "go native" in them. Ironically, develop and feel more secure about my own point of view or traditions. It is the secure person who feels less threatened by difference. Shift corporate culture from its present motivational position of *fear*.

Diversity Check
- Do you relate easily to people who are different from yourself?
- At a party, do you reach out to meet new people rather than chatting to those you already know?
- Do you feel there is more than one way to solve a problem or reach a goal?
- When having a conversation with people you disagree with, can you see their side of the issue?

Field Independence

Once during his long campaign for Indian independence, Mahatma Gandhi organized a national march from one side of India to the other. Tens of thousands walked with him in the dust and heat. Midway through, he suddenly stopped and announced, "No, No, this is a mistake! Turn back." Appalled, his followers questioned his judgment and consistency. Gandhi replied, "My commitment is not to consistency. My commitment is to do what I think is right at every moment, even if it means saying that I was wrong."

Field independence is a psychological term that means being able to stand against the crowd or, as in Gandhi's case, even against the previous dictates of my own mind. It is to have my own firm convictions that I live by, even if these isolate me or make me unpopular. It is to know my own mind and to be able to hold my own point of view, despite group pressure. More subtly, it is to see through and stand against the currents of my organization or culture that would influence my independent judgment, and to be able to stand apart from immediate circumstances and see my own way through.

More difficult still, field independence implies an ability to stand apart from the paradigms or habitual patterns of my own mind, to see when I am in error or thinking in boxes. Even more subtly, it means to be deeply independent of entanglement, of those tendencies in my own being that might imprison me—craving, hating, resenting, envying, a need for flattery or justification, the thrill of popularity. These are all things that influence my reactions and responses and that trap me lower down on the scale of motivations.

At its most spiritual, to be field-independent is to stand on a high mountain in the clear air and have a wide, independent perspective. To have the strength to be lonely, to feel isolated, to feel that I am the only person on the planet who sees as I do—and yet carry on. It is to be steady, focused, steadfast, independent-minded, self-critical, dedicated, and committed. These are qualities necessary in the captain of a (corporate?) ship sailing a wild sea or the officer who must take command in the midst of battle. They are also the qualities of the scientist or the artist (or any innovator) who discovers a new way of seeing or doing something. Field-independent people can seem stubborn, they can be genuinely subversive, but without them ideas and culture never move forward. The herd is always led by someone who can stand apart from the herd.

Opposites: Conventional or suggestible people are the opposite of field-independent. They need the support of the group, the support of tradition or convention. A person who depends on approval, on the good opinion of others, or who is overly dependent on circumstances cannot be field-independent. Also, anyone who is blind to their own temptations and motivations (lacking self-awareness) cannot be self-critical or truly disciplined.

Common Distortions: The philosopher Nietzsche said, "convictions are more dangerous enemies of truth than lies." Men or women of conviction can be just plain stubborn. They can be fanatical, unreceptive to criticism, obstinate, closed to other points of view or to diversity. Perhaps worst of all, they can believe in themselves too much and become immune to self-criticism.

How to Nurture: A practice of daily meditation or reflection that cultivates self-awareness will help develop field independence. Reflect on my own deepest values and on what it takes to live true to them. Check myself at the end of the day: Did I give way to flattery or a need for approval? Was I reluctant to fight for my point of view? Did I brush aside the criticism of others or fail to be vigilant about my own motives?

Field Independence Check
  • Are you willing to stand by your convictions
    when all around you disagree?
  • Are you willing to be unpopular in a good cause?
  • Do you dress to please yourself instead of others?
  • Do you enjoy your own company?
  • Do you consider carefully and listen to others
    before going your own way?

Asking Why?

A few years ago a very serious accident struck a Japanese
nuclear power plant. The flow of coolant through the reactor decreased and the control rods overheated. The reactor reached criticality and exploded. In the inquiry that
followed it was discovered that engineers at the plant had
taken a shortcut in an effort to boost the plant's efficiency.
Not understanding the fundamental principles of a nuclear
reactor, they caused an accident. The engineers forgot to
ask, Why?

The natural curiosity of children makes them repeat
"Why?" incessantly, yet in both our schools and in our
organizations we discourage questions. Questions are
seen as bothersome, distracting, even disloyal. Children
attend school to be taught; employees (and even managers) are hired who will be told what to do. The result
of this is to discourage not just the child in us (the passion, freshness, and spontaneity) but also the creativity
of the childlike questions that have accompanied all
great adult innovations and breakthroughs. Isaac Newton
famously described himself as being like a young boy
standing on a beach in awe of the great ocean of undis-
covered truth that lay before him. Einstein, when asked
about the secret of his great intelligence, answered,

"When I was a young boy in school I used to get into trouble for asking so many questions. Now that I am a famous scientist, I am allowed to ask all the questions I like, even 'dumb' ones."

An active curiosity and a tendency to ask fundamental Why? questions are critical to the whole scientific spirit, which is a spirit of endless inquiry. In quantum science, Heisenberg's famous Uncertainty Principle established that asking questions (doing experiments) actually creates reality. Questions pluck possibilities from the infinite sea of potentiality (the quantum vacuum) and turn them into actualities. Yet we see that our corporate culture, drenched as it is in an atmosphere of fear, has little tolerance for questions. As a result it represses the higher motivations of exploration and creativity.

A need to ask Why? stems from our deeper motivation to understand things, to get to the bottom of them (*exploration*). It is accompanied by a tendency to refuse to take anything for granted, questioning the reasons, foundations, or inner workings of everything, and asking if it could be better or different. Asking Why? also takes us beyond the given, the present situation, and encourages us to explore the future. Why do we make this product rather than that one? Why do we use this distribution system or these raw materials instead of some others? Such questions are necessary to innovation and growth. And they allow us to thrive on uncertainty because we are not so frightened of moving on.

The critics are right to fear this penchant for Why? questions. Questions are subversive. They usually question the status quo. They undermine smug assumptions and prejudices and rock the boat. The boat they rock may be my own. Thus the price of good questions is a willingness to question my own assumptions, values, and methods as well as those of others. This of course requires humility (reducing *self-assertion*). It also requires making that same quantum leap about the infinite nature of truth that is required by the celebration of diversity. I must see that truth is infinite before I can cultivate a tendency to keep looking for more behind any "answer," to maintain a preference for good questions over good answers. This can make you a player of the infinite game, one who plays with boundaries rather than within them. (Can you imagine a corporate CEO who says to young executives, "I want you to come in here tomorrow morning with ten good questions, ten things that you don't understand"?)

Opposites: People who don't ask fundamental questions either lack curiosity or they are fearful. The lack of questions leads to a lack of deep involvement, to passivity and perhaps to an unquestioning gullibility. A reluctance to ask questions may also arise from conformity or lack of initiative.

Common Distortions: Like all good things, a tendency to ask questions can be taken too far. It can show an inclination to undermine others, or to be "clever." Too many questions can also make people indecisive or vacillating, afraid to take any action because they can see so many alternatives. (*Hamlet*: "To be sicklied o'er with the pale cast of thought.")

How to Nurture: Encourage questions from myself and others, be open to challenge, and always look for "the matter behind the matter," the further truth or possibility behind any answer or explanation. Reward questions in others, encourage them to probe. Pay attention to surprising or anomalous events or facts—they are clues to seeing things from a wholly new perspective. (Scientific revolutions always follow from incorporating anomalies that a previous science could not explain.)

Why? Check

- Do you try to understand the meaning behind rules, customs, and events?
- Are you dissatisfied with first explanations?
- Do you like to glean the thinking behind other people's pronouncements, to understand "where they are coming from"?
- Do you sometimes reflect on cultural or behavioral trends and wonder why they are as they are?
- Do you like to keep up to date with current affairs?

Reframing

Peter Schwartz's *Art of the Long View* and the work on scenario planning at Royal/Dutch Shell that it describes have transformed strategic thinking. The essence of that transformation is an ability to rethink the past and to imagine the future—indeed, to imagine many possible futures, and to see how these might bear on present decision making. Both rethinking the past and imagining the future are acts of reframing—literally, putting a different (larger, broader) frame around a situation or problem and then seeing it from a larger or different perspective.

Reframing requires standing back from a situation, suggestion, strategy, or problem and looking for the bigger picture, the wider context. Sometimes this wider context is spatial, taking in a wider geographic perspective or a wider set of people and situations likely to be influenced by a decision. Sometimes it is temporal, noticing how different a strategy looks if viewed over a longer time frame. Some solutions to problems look brilliant in the short term, but if looked at from a long-term perspective they seem quite dumb. Vandana Shiva has pointed out that the World Bank's policy of dumping industrial pollutants in Third World countries is such a dumb solution. Over the long term, the overall contamination of the earth's atmosphere is the same, and will affect us all, wherever on the globe we initially dump the pollutants. The same criticism can be made of President Bush's rejection of the Kyoto Treaty. To claim that saving the earth's environment "is not in America's interests" is to view those interests in a very narrow time frame.

Perhaps the most critical block to reframing problems (or opportunities) is our own minds, the fact that most of us are always thinking inside some box, inside some set of assumptions. We have first to become conscious of this and of what these assumptions are, and then we have to blow up (or blow out) the walls of the box. This can take us into our discomfort zones. As Peter Schwartz describes the process at Shell, "We evolved a discipline that allowed us to examine our mind-sets so that we could bring forth our prejudices and assumptions. . . . But what helped focus our attention on useful subjects was paying attention to those situations that made us uncomfortable or which we really did not understand."

People (and organizations) that can reframe are more visionary, able to imagine (and perhaps bring about) futures that do not yet exist. Hence they are open to possibilities. They are creative (seeing the not yet seen) and broad in outlook. They are of necessity self-critical, and usually more adventurous. But because they can see beyond their own and others' paradigms, their insights can feel threatening or "mad" to those more comfortable with the given or with the narrow view. This has always been true in science and the arts as well as business.

Psychologists have found that it is possible to predict which adolescents and adults will be better at reframing situations from their behavior as small children. In one experiment, four-year-olds were offered two marshmallows, with the proviso that they could have two more later if they only ate one of these now. When retested at the age of fourteen, those children who had been able to delay their gratification at age four now showed wider and more sophisticated cognitive abilities, including an ability to reframe.[2] An overall strength of character embeds many of these qualities of spiritual intelligence.

At the spiritual level, reframing can be seen as bringing something new into the world or something new into yourself. In this sense, reframing your set of assumptions can be like undergoing an act of initiation.

Opposites: The person or organization that cannot reframe problems or opportunities is always fighting bushfires. Caught in a narrow perspective, people see only the here and now. They are too focused or hidebound and suffer from "paradigm paralysis."

Common Distortions: Too many headlines and not enough substance. Too much "vision" while impatient with detail and unable to deal with practical matters. Lost in possibilities. Sometimes a rebellious need to challenge existing assumptions even when these are adequate for the moment.

How to Nurture: Build a set of conceptual models that contextualize a problem or issue, and make each model more comprehensive (larger) than the last. Subject assumptions to criticism by exposure to other points of view. Hold brainstorming sessions with unconventional people. Participate in regular dialogue groups. Think the "impossible" and see how it feels. Just finding my current position on the scale of motivations and comparing it to where I (or my organization) want to be can initiate an act of reframing.

Reframing Check
- Are you good at looking at questions from many angles?
- Do you go outside your comfort zone when seeking new experiences?
- Do you "cast your net wide" for information that might bear on the problem at hand? That is, do you go outside the box?
- Do you question the value of things' being left just as they are?
- Are you good at seeing the big picture?

The Positive Use of Adversity

Charles Handy describes an "alchemist" as somebody who can make things happen, someone who can create something out of nothing. Such people are the innovators in business, the arts, and the sciences. A common feature of alchemists is their "doggedness," their ability to stick with a project or an idea and see it through no matter how tough or disaster-ridden it gets. "Alchemists have the extraordinary ability," says Handy, "to turn disaster into new life."[3]

One of Handy's alchemists is Virgin's Richard Branson, a man who even did a brief stint in jail for one of his early business mistakes. Says Branson, "My businesses grow out of my experiences, usually my bad experiences. I see something done badly which I know that we could do better—like the airline." Like all English schoolboys, Branson would have grown up with Rudyard Kipling's character-forming poem, "If": "If you can meet with triumph and disaster and treat those two imposters just the same . . . then you will be a man, my son." Positive use of adversity is an important quality of spiritual intelligence because it enables us to learn from and use our mistakes. It teaches us to recognize our limits, not just to live within them but often to surpass them. We grow and learn from suffering or failure and make gains from our setbacks. "Pick myself up, dust myself off, and start all over again." Yet such wisdom goes against the grain of a corporate culture that takes no prisoners: "Here is your budget," say most senior managers. "It is tight, so don't make any mistakes." I know of no corporation that gives an award for the most creative mistake of the week. Rather the ethos is *screw up, and you pay for it*. This is one of the chief reasons an atmosphere of fear permeates corporate culture.

The positive use of adversity requires great strength of character, but it is also the only thing that really builds character. "That which does not kill me makes me stronger," said the German philosopher Nietzsche. Using adversity requires the courage to look at my own weaknesses, faults and past mistakes, to own them, learn from them, and grow beyond them. It requires that I be brave enough to face the pain that accompanies shame, and thus have the resilience to grow beyond the causes of that shame. As American sociologist Richard Sennett points out, this in turn requires that I have an underlying and abiding sense of self, a sense of self that transcends the short-term working experiences, flexible institutions, and constant risk-taking that characterize corporate culture.[4] Such a sense of self can arise only from living true to my deepest values. Sennett calls this "fidelity to oneself."

More subtly, the positive use of adversity requires recognition of the tragic truth that not all problems have solutions, not all differences can be resolved—and yet you need the ability to carry on just the same. (To be able to bear, as Shakespeare describes it, that elusive sadness that lies at the heart of the creative.) Such recognition confers a deep wisdom and maturity, a sense of having made my peace with life, or at least of having given life a good run for its money. To fly in the face of tragedy or setback in turn helps to build a basic trust in life, and thus a greater ability to live with uncertainty.

Opposites: Those who cannot make a positive use of adversity usually fall back on self-pity, feeling victimized or placing the blame on others. The corporate liking for scapegoats who can be blamed or fired is symptomatic of this. An inability to deal with failure or suffering leads to despair and a sense of defeat. These can lead to the further damage of a permanent defensiveness or cynicism rather than to healing. It can lead to making the same mistake again and again.

Common Distortions: Taken too far, a stiff upper lip can lead to a stony stoicism, to a loss of vulnerability and hence a loss of openness. The courage to be vulnerable is also necessary to growth and creativity. A reluctance to be defeated by fortune can also lead to recklessness sparked by a misplaced belief that I can overcome anything, that nothing can ever touch me.

How to Nurture: Sennett's advice is best on this. To develop deep resilience we must cultivate a deep sense of self, a deep awareness of our most fundamental values and the sense of a focal point or compass within. These in turn are nurtured by daily meditation and reflection. Getting in touch with that inner place that survives the ephemeral, the impermanent, finding—with Archimedes—a fulcrum on which to rest the lever that will move the world.

Use of Adversity Check
- Do you learn from and grow beyond past failures?
- When bad things happen to you, do you find some way to carry on despite them?
- Do you bounce back reasonably quickly from periods of gloom or dark depression?
- Does the loss of certainties lead you to a deeper faith or vision?
- Do you find some reason to cling to ideals despite all the evil and mess in the world?

Humility

The director of executive education at a major international business school criticized my list of the twelve processes of SQ for including humility. "Businesspeople aren't very interested in being humble these days," she argued. Yet humility is described in the *Harvard Business Review* as one of two essential defining qualities of a "Level 5 Leader"—one who can "transform a good company into a great one . . . [a catalyst who can] elevate companies from mediocrity to sustained excellence."[5] The other defining quality of a Level 5 Leader is possession of a fierce resolve.

A sense of humility, or modesty, raises our motivations and responses into the positive zone of higher motivations. It gets us beyond the isolation of and preoccupation with our own egos and assumed self-importance. It opens up the possibility of learning from others and from experience. People who think of themselves as God's gift to the world and as knowing more than anyone else have little motive to listen or learn.

Healthy humility gives me a sense that I am but one player in a larger drama and makes me more aware of the good qualities and achievements of others. It makes me aware how much my own achievements are grounded on those of others and on the gifts and good fortune that life has thrown my way. This, in turn, makes me more sensitive to the needs of others, and more likely to be a leader who creates space where others can realize their own best talents. It makes me ask questions and seek advice, and gives me a readiness to admit that I could be wrong and others could be right. This promotes a healthy self-criticism and makes me both aware of and ready to admit my own limits. It also prevents me from taking myself too seriously.

At a more spiritual level, a sense of humility puts us in touch with a sense that our true importance comes from something deeper than, or from something beyond, our mere ego selves. Beyond a purely secular sense of "knowing my place" in the natural and social worlds, it helps my self-awareness evolve into seeing myself as a part of humanity, a part of the universe, as a child of God, or as an excitation in the common field of energy shared by all. It provides a wider context and deeper meaning for my life. This makes humility a companion of gratitude, of deeper self-awareness, and of a wish to serve. Very great leaders like Abraham Lincoln, Mahatma Gandhi, and

Nelson Mandela have all combined deep personal humility with great political vision and fierce resolve.

Opposites: An absence of humility leads of course to too much pride and to overbearing arrogance. It leads to a domineering or even a grandiose style of leadership that discourages or belittles others and their motivation. Such self-love or self-adulation can lead to deep loneliness. It is also a large contributing factor in fanaticism. Fanatics wrongly believe that they have an exclusive access to truth. In business as well as politics and religion this can lead to dogma, blinkered vision, and often to disaster. Lack of humility can also impede good strategic thinking. Arrogant executives are less open to any information that does not support their existing view or existing strategy.

Common Distortions: All good things can be taken too far or distorted. The obsequiousness of Charles Dickens's Uriah Heep gives us the shivers. Less extremely, distorted humility can lead to self-doubt, low self-esteem, indecisiveness, or even to shame. It can make us give way when we shouldn't. Healthy humility is always underpinned by a healthy self-respect and sense of self-worth.

How to Nurture: Reflect on how much I owe to others, or to life's circumstances. Who or what has helped to make me *me?* Day by day, or situation by situation, reflect on what others have contributed. From whom or what did I learn today? When were there times that I seemed to need appreciation or even flattery? Why? What qualms or bad feeling did I have about myself that made me need others to bolster my ego? What strengths can I find in myself that make me less vulnerable to the judgments of others?

Humility Check
- Are you happy to recognize that you are but one player in a larger drama?
- If you make a mistake, can you admit it gracefully?
- Do you think that your importance comes from something larger than yourself? That you owe your gifts to a deeper or higher source?
- Do you remain open to the suggestions and contributions of others, even if they take you by surprise?
- Do you accept that you have limitations, that there is only so much that you can or should do?

A Sense of Vocation

A British fashion designer told me she thought there were three reasons that someone might start a business. The first reason, she said, was just that there is an exploitable hole in the market. "You see that something is wanted or needed, and you decide to provide it." The second reason is personal opportunity—inheriting a business from your family, or having a special skill or talent to provide a certain kind of thing, like fashion design or sound systems. "But the third reason is different," she said. "The third reason for starting a business is just a sense of I have to, it just has to be." This third reason is more visionary, a felt need to bring something into the world.

A sense of vocation is the active accompaniment to having a vision. It is a desire and the will to make that vision come true. Literally from the Latin word *vocare*, "to be called," a vocation originally meant a call to take up holy orders, to be called by God. As an SQ quality, I mean it as any calling to higher service, a sense of being called upon to make something good or beautiful happen in this world. It is a call to pursue a certain course in life, a sense of deep personal (transpersonal!) purpose, a need to act from and act upon your deepest ideals and values. Teaching and medicine have traditionally been viewed as vocations; the law, at its most ideal, is one too. The ideal posed by the paradigm of spiritual capital is that being a business leader should also become a vocation.

A sense of vocation is far deeper than merely having an ambition or a goal. There is no vocation in saying, "I want to be a millionaire by the time I am thirty." Rather, having a sense of vocation is being driven by a wish to make my life useful, by a strong need to make a difference. It often comes from following an inspiration. It need not be a grand vocation like saving the world. A person can be called to become an honest leader, a good parent, or an active citizen. The essential quality is that "*it has to be.*"

A sense of vocation usually follows from a deep sense of gratitude, a sense that I have been given very much and now I want to give something back. That something I wish to give is not used or intended to manipulate those whom I will serve. It is a gift. Beyond mere gratitude, this quality may arise from a sense of reverence, reverence for the existence of some quality or example, or even for the gift of life itself. The Trappist monastic order has as its motto *Laborare est orare,* "to work is to pray." Their reverence for God's works leads its members to work in the world.

People who feel a sense of vocation are usually thoughtful and quite grounded. They feel at peace with life and have a deep sense of belonging. They often have a quality of radiance or vitality that can inspire others. They are generous not just with their work but with themselves—with their time and their deep engagement.

Opposites: I am unlikely to feel a sense of vocation if I just take others' and life's gifts for granted. I have no motive or wish to give anything back. I may just want to get by in life. I may be preoccupied with furthering my own patch, or even bitter, wishing to give life "a good kick in the teeth." I can't have a sense of vocation if I am suffering from *anomie,* a sense that I have no meaningful role to play in life.

Common Distortions: Taken out of proportion or too seriously, a sense of vocation can give rise to anxiety. I may even feel guilty that I am not doing enough. I may become a fanatic, or I may practice poor judgment because I lose sight of my own limitations.

How to Nurture: Reflect on how much I have (and how much others don't have). Reflect on what my life would be like without its basic gifts (health, sunshine, love, and the rest). Make a point of thanking people, or the source of all my gifts (God?), inwardly or outwardly. Pass on something that was given to me by passing on a gift to others, some help, a start in life, an opportunity, a loan, even a smile. Reflect on what really moves and motivates me and explore how I can use that to make a difference.

Sense of Vocation Check
- Do you feel that you want your life to "make a difference"?
- When someone does you a favor, do you feel you should pass a gift on to the next person?

- Do you feel called upon to repay all the good things that have been given to you in life?
- Do you feel a sense of responsibility to others, the community, or the world that goes beyond your official duty or commitments?
- Do you feel your life has a sense of direction that you should follow?

A Psychometric Instrument?

It is always interesting to know whether something like spiritual intelligence can be tested for. While the kind of objective scoring used for IQ measurement seems both impossible and inappropriate, it might be possible to use the twelve qualities distinctive of SQ to devise a useful assessment instrument. Ian Marshall and I did devise one such questionnaire, and have piloted it on three groups of executives attending one or another of our workshops.

The questionnaire consisted of eighty-four items, seven for each of the twelve qualities. Most of these items were identical to questions that appear in the "Check" section of each quality just described, though they were scrambled to make it less easy to second-guess appropriate answers. In all the questionnaire was given to seventy-one people and then subjected to statistical analysis. Three particularly interesting conclusions emerged from this small experiment:

- The average scores of all three executive groups were very similar, and markedly higher than the scores of a randomly selected group of administrative staff. This suggests the pilot test may be a useful measuring instrument.

- The scores on each of the individual twelve qualities had medium-sized correlations with each other. The twelve subtests of the SQ qualities were not measuring exactly the same thing, nor totally different things. They are best seen as measuring twelve aspects of a single quality, which we defined as SQ. More than half (52 percent) of the total variance on the twelve qualities was contained in one number: the total score on the test.
- The SQ assessment scores achieved bore no relation to gender, that is, we saw no significant difference between the scores of men and women. The scores on SQ also bore no relation to Myers-Briggs personality type, suggesting that SQ is an independent factor.

These were very preliminary results, but they suggest that further research using the twelve SQ qualities as measurement criteria might gain positive results.

8

How Shift Happens

As a young child I was a bright, straight-A student. But by the age of thirteen, I was apathetic and lost. I had no interest in anything, I had put on weight, had spots on my face, and got straight C's on my report card. School seemed a waste of time; life itself just a succession of dull, gray, pointless days. I actually considered suicide. It was my life's first big crisis. My parents were of no use. I had lost faith in my family some time before. All they could do was fight. Religion couldn't help me. I had lost my faith in Christianity at the age of eleven and it seemed certain I would never feel such passion again.

I was jolted out of my crisis by two events. The first was a stunning lecture by my junior high school science teacher on the atom and nuclear physics. The teacher brought in colorful models, including a model of a nuclear reactor with moving parts. He told us how atomic bombs were made. Before that lecture I found science very boring. But now it seemed to hold out a whole new world of mystery, awe, and power, a tiny micro-world we could only imagine with its own quirky quantum laws and relationships that were beyond the imagination. I literally ran home from school filled with excitement and demanded to be taken to a bookstore.

The other event, which happened within two weeks of my discovering the atom, was the Russian launch of Sputnik. That was the first satellite to orbit the earth successfully, and it sent a tide of fear through the American psyche. We were behind in the space race, the Russians were leaping ahead in science, and they would eventually use their superiority to conquer us. In a flash of insight my own life, and the motives that drove it, shifted radically. America needed scientists. I was now interested in atomic physics. I would become an atomic scientist to serve my country. That pivotal shift has directed the whole central thread of my life ever since, taking me into a passion for quantum physics, a university career in physics and philosophy at MIT, and then writing my books about the impact of the quantum vision on psychology, management, and spirituality. The motive to serve America has shifted to the wider motive of wishing to serve humanity, or the future, but the central theme remains the same. "I," as I now know myself to be, was born in that two-week period straddling the two events that shook me out of my apathy and fear at age thirteen.

I tell my personal story because it illustrates vividly how a person can be stuck in lower motivations (-4, *fear,* and -6, *apathy*) but then undergo a sudden shift to higher ones ($+4$, *mastery*—of the physics and its philosophy—and $+6$, *higher service*). The shift in this personal case was brought about through two of the transformative principles of spiritual intelligence coming to bear on my life and original motives. It was as though they had shot my life full of sudden new energy. These were the principles of *positive use of adversity* (turning my patriotic fear into a mastery of physics), and *sense of vocation* (turning my apathy into a heartfelt wish to serve my country). This personal case of SQ shift is part of a larger map or pattern illustrated in Figure 8.1.

This chart, where twelve of the sixteen motives that drive human behavior are correlated with the twelve processes of change that give SQ its active qualities, reveals the particular dynamic that shifted the course of my own life. The chart also provides a first hint of how other such shifts could happen, to individuals or to cultures. It is the central visual image of this book and summarizes the way the book can be used to alter human behavior. It also summarizes the different natures and roles of motives and SQ processes, and how the dynamic between them results in long-term cultural and behavioral shift.

To recap earlier observations, motives are attractors in the shared field of consciousness or meaning. They are just energy states, not consciously chosen. Energy is distributed among them—reaching equilibrium scattered among these states. By contrast, SQ qualities require acts of consciousness and will. They can be freely chosen. They have the force to pump energy into the motivational states, and to redistribute human energies into higher-energy motivational states (into new attractors). To get a concrete image of all this, think back to the earlier example of the steel balls and gullies in a pinball machine, illustrated here in Figure 8.2. The gullies in the pinball machine are the motivational attractors, energy states into which we (the steel balls) can sink. The SQ transformation processes enter the stable pinball system when we pull back the spring and shoot a new ball (new energy) into the system. This new energy can move the existing balls out of their gullies into new, higher-valued ones.

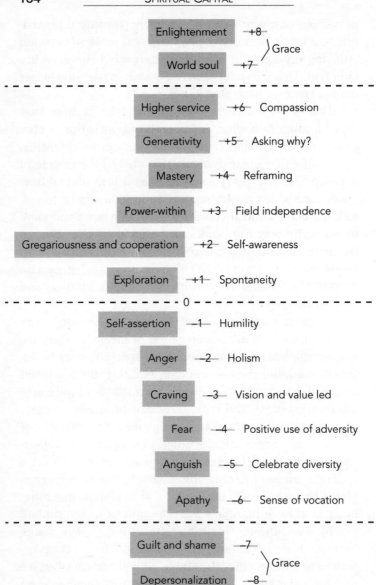

Figure 8.1 *How SQ Processes Act on Motives*

Figure 8.2 *The Pinball Machine of Life*

In my personal example, it was a *sense of vocation* (SQ process) that shifted my underlying motivation from −6, *apathy,* to +6, *higher service.* Other such shifts are easy to see on the chart. For instance, the SQ process *humility* could shift a motive from −1, *self-assertion* to +1, *exploration,* and a sense of *holism* (seeing the deeper pattern, all the interconnections) could shift a person's motive from −2, *anger* to +2, *cooperation.* The chart can provide more insight into the full dynamics of possible shift, but first it is necessary to understand the basic conditions required to make shift possible.

The Role of Crisis

Fossil records show that for the first 99 percent of the life of a species, it is stable. For the last 1 percent, when it has presumably hit an environmental crisis, it becomes unstable. It suddenly produces many mutations in all directions, some of which may survive the crisis as new species. It is the same with human beings and organizations. We spend most of our time in an ordered, habitual state, going about our activities in the same way we always have. Whatever motives drive us are also stable 99 percent of the time. The world couldn't really carry on if this were not the case. Creativity is desirable but costly. It takes as much energy per unit of time to have a creative thought as it does to play a game of rugby football. Bringing any SQ transformative process into play to shift motives means pumping energy into the system. That energy has to come from somewhere.

Shifting the qualities or position of a stable system requires enormous energy, but during that 1 percent of the time the system is evolving, things are different. When a stable system meets a crisis, it can move to the edge of chaos (become radically unstable). At the edge of chaos, elements of the system are less stuck. It is as though, on a pinball machine, the gullies holding the steel balls have suddenly become much shallower. Now when new energy (a new ball) is shot into the system, the existing balls fly out of their gullies much more easily, and in all directions. The balls are searching for new attractors (new gullies) into which they can fall. This is what happens to a human being or to an organization in crisis—it takes less energy to shift the underlying motivations that have been directing behavior. So bringing SQ to bear on a system in crisis is more likely to be effective than using it to shift a stable situation.

Here are some common examples of how crisis can move people to the point of changing their behavior. A man whose very bad temper upsets his wife may do nothing to restrain himself until one day his wife leaves him. An alcoholic will seldom give up drink until his whole life has reached a state of crisis—he loses his job, loses his wife, is told his liver won't last another year. People seldom change their behavior unless they have to. Shifting behavior requires shifting underlying motives, that is, shifting a whole paradigm. We only garner the energy to shift paradigms when our old paradigm isn't working.

At a steel plant in the north of England where I worked as a consultant, the impending crisis promised the imminent closure of the plant and the loss of twelve hundred jobs. The way this crisis unfolded, and the paradigms that had to be shifted, offers a good example of SQ transformation processes at work in shifting motives.

The steel plant in question had a long history of labor-management strife. Given the constraints of the English class system, the workers and their union leaders were working-class men while the managers were middle class. This alone laid firm foundations for strife and mistrust. But in addition the plant was not doing well. Competition from Eastern Europe had cut into profits. Indeed, the mill was currently running at a loss. Despite this, the unions would not consider wage cuts or changes in working practices. Both sides of the conflict just blamed each other, and civil communication between them had all but ceased. To top it all off, the parent company had brought in a new female CEO from the United States to try to turn the situation around. Aside from tea ladies and the occasional secretary, she was the only woman at the site. English working-class men do not easily abide being told what to do by a woman, particularly an American one.

Looking at the possible motivations on the chart, it's easy to see that both management and workers at the steel mill were stuck on the negative part of the scale. Management and union bosses were maintaining their right to call the shots (−1, *self-assertion*). There was incredible *anger* (−2) on both sides. Management wanted more power and higher profits and the unions wanted easy working conditions and better wages (−3, *craving*). Both sides also craved security. There was also a great deal of *fear* (−4)—on both sides—that the plant would be closed. For some of the workers at the plant, who had known no other jobs since the age of sixteen, fear of closure had even led to a certain amount of *anguish,* −5. By the time the consultants were called in, this was a plant in deep crisis.

After the usual period of analysis, our consultancy group decided that poor communication, lack of trust, and blinkered vision were the main enemies of cooperation at the mill. Without cooperation, the mill had no future and its twelve hundred people would be joining the unemployed. After consulting all the various warring groups separately, we settled on the establishment of a dialogue group as our first strategy. This was to be dialogue of the sort first articulated by the physicist David Bohm and then further developed by Bill Isaacs' Dialogue Group at MIT. Representative members of the steel mill's community, from furnace workers and fore-men to division managers and the CEO herself were asked to attend the dialogue group regularly. All were asked to speak plainly and honestly while avoiding personal rudeness, and to speak without fear. There were to be no unwanted consequences of what went on in the group.

In this dialogue group, men spoke to each other across the usual barriers of job description or status. They spoke about issues that had never been openly discussed, and how they felt about them. It emerged that *everyone* was full of fear, and no one wanted to see the mill close. The conversations around this, where warring factions came to see each others' points of view (*holism*), itself shifted group motivations from −2, *anger* to +2, *cooperation,* and then by means of the acquired *humility,* from −1, *self-assertion,* to the more useful and positive +1, *exploration.* But the biggest shift of all was brought about through qualities driving the CEO.

Instead of avoiding confrontation or pretending to have all the answers, this petite blond American woman spoke out honestly. She pointed out that it wasn't easy being the only female on the plant site, nor the only American in that area of England. She, too, found the situation awkward. But most strikingly of all, the CEO confessed she was as fearful as everyone else. She couldn't be certain the transformation plans designed to save the mill would work (*humility*). All they together could do was make the best of a very bad situation (*positive use of adversity*). They might have to remodel their whole notion of how the plant should function (*reframing*). Though expressing her uncertainty about the future, the CEO spoke with authority and inner conviction (+4, *mastery*).

In this particular case, the dynamics of the dialogue group itself brought into play nearly all twelve of the transformative process of SQ. This was managed in part by the facilitators' directing the conversation so as to evoke those processes in participants, and in part just because that is what good dialogue does. The shift in the motives that drove the mill's culture also owed much to the new CEO's own higher motivation of *mastery*. When an organization is led by someone at least as high as *mastery*, its whole culture is moved toward higher motivations. For the steel mill it worked brilliantly. Within six months, the issues of communication, trust, and vision were cleared up, and all the people at the plant put their backs into making the company's transformation program work. Camaraderie at the plant increased tenfold, across class, status, and gender divides. The mill took one more year to return to profitability.

The crisis at the steel mill worked out in part simply because it was a crisis. Before the entrenched negative motivations driving the mill's culture had come to crisis point (imminent plant closure), the semblance of stability ensured that the situation remained stagnant. It was only when it seemed all was about to be lost that the people at the mill cried out for help. The mill was then in a state of radical instability poised at the edge of chaos. It now had the potential of a complex adaptive system. Shift was going to be possible if wisely directed.

Further Dynamics of Shift

In Figure 8.1, individual SQ processes are aligned with the individual motives. That can give a very biased, almost Newtonian interpretation of how SQ influences motivation. It is true that one-on-one shift does often happen, and when it does, two different degrees of motivational change are possible. If influenced by *holism,* a person or a group motivated by *anger* (−2), can make a "quantum leap" to the opposite, positive quality of +2, *cooperation.* The steelworkers at the mill made that sort of move. But under the influence of *holism,* a person might equally well make the smaller shift from −2, *anger* to −1, *self-assertion.*

One-on-one influence is only one way, however, that the SQ processes can shift motivation. This kind of shift is, if you like, the "particle-like" aspect of SQ transformational energy. It behaves rather like one billiard ball hitting another and transferring energy to it. But SQ energy also has a "wave-like" aspect, resembling ripples on a pond (the field of meaning). In this more wave-like way of influencing things, several, or all, of the SQ processes can come to bear on a motivation or motivational complex. It is as though the individual or the group has become generally open to the whole SQ phenomenon. In this case, the holistic nature of the SQ processes, the fact that each process is rather like a fractal that contains within itself all the other processes, becomes evident. The British steel mill's dialogue group brought into play at least the linked SQ processes of *humility, holism, positive use of adversity, spontaneity, self-awareness,* and *reframing.* It was the gestalt, or pattern, of energy input that raised the group's motivational level.

There are most likely dozens of ways to work with the SQ transformation principles to bring about desired motivational—and hence individual or cultural—shifts. This is a new field of psychology and motivation theory that yet has much to discover. But it's useful to look in some detail at the two most classic ways that SQ can influence motivational change—the one-on-one, particle-like sort of shift and the more general, wave-like sort of shift. The salient features of each can be seen, in turn, in a one-on-one counseling or mentoring session, contrasted with a discussion of the dynamics of the dialogue group.

A One-on-One Counseling Session

This case is an abbreviated report of a counseling session from the practice case notes of Ian Marshall. All the conversation reported took place in just one forty-minute session. It was the client's first session with Marshall. It was recorded, and is published with the client's permission.

The client was a highly intelligent widower in his mid-fifties. He was Jewish, of Middle European origin. He was an office worker who also did some writing in his spare time. When he arrived at Marshall's office he was dressed in an almost ostentatiously disheveled fashion, with a long, baggy, and not very clean overcoat and longish, unkempt hair. He had brought several parcels in brown paper bags with him to the interview, and he continually rearranged these around his feet as the conversation proceeded.

This man had come for counseling because he felt his life was being dominated by feelings of antagonism, and that by letting them upset him so much, he had let other people gain too much control over his life. Marshall had given him Cattell's Sixteen Personality Factor Test (the "16-PF") the week before, and knew that the man scored very highly on intelligence, anxiety, guilt proneness, and frustration. Marshall placed him at -2, *anger,* on the Scale of Motivations.

Marshall began by asking this client about his week, and whether anything in particular had caused him to feel antagonism. This allowed him to become a sort of audio witness to a sea of incidents and woes that had upset the client—his boss, people who had wronged him in the past, his mother, his landlords. His voice filled with anger, and he confessed that nothing would make him feel better but revenge. "I spend a lot of my time thinking about revenge." The counselor then asked him to pick out one particular incident or person that most upset him that week.

"My landlords," he finally answered. "They're always picking fights with me, always cheating me, and this week they wouldn't listen to me." He detailed several alleged cheats with the electricity meter, the gas meter, a disagreement about rent money, and then complained at some length about "being overlooked as a person. For them, I just don't exist."

At this point the counselor attempted to bring some understanding to factors underlying his client's anger by directing him toward getting a broader picture of it (*holism*). The client focused on his landlords' making him feel small and worthless ("not listening to me, not trusting me") and his voice soon changed from rasping antagonism and a bit of whining to a more assertive tone. Under the influence of *holism,* he shifted from −2, *anger,* to −1, *self-assertion*. He then spent several minutes assuring Marshall (and indirectly his landlords) of his own worth: "I am a human being in my own right. I am the king of my castle. I don't care what they think."

Next the counselor nudged his client gently with *humility*. Could he be a big enough person to rise above all this bickering? Could he see any wider context for his daily squabbles with his landlords? The client soon came to the insight that he was letting little things bother him too much and began to explore why. That reflected a shift from −1, *self-assertion,* to +1, *exploration*. The conversation proceeded along those lines for several minutes, then the counselor asked the client how he felt about his landlords at that point. Did he have any new response to them (*spontaneity*)? The client fell into a long silence, as though going through images in his head. Finally, he said in a low, almost gentle tone, "Poor bastard. The husband. He's crippled and confined to a wheelchair. No wonder he just sits around stewing about little things all day. It's him I should be feeling sorry for." At this point, the client has shifted again, from +1, *exploration* to +2, *cooperation,* a feeling of some empathy and compassion for his landlord. He commented that he no longer felt angry with him, and in general felt better.

This was a very dramatic series of shifts for one interview, and had to be reinforced and sustained by further sessions on other upsetting topics. But after eighteen months of counseling, the client had become more relaxed and confident, had begun to sharpen up his appearance, and soon after, remarried.

The Dialogue Group

The dialogue process is the most effective way known to bring about deep motivational shift and the resulting behavioral change in a group or an organizational culture. The dialogue circle itself acts as a container for the field of meaning common to the group, and thus exposes the group's collective and individual motivations (and attitudes) to the twelve transformational processes of SQ. In this case, the SQ processes act more as a diffuse, wave-like, and interconnected whole, energizing many levels of participants' consciousness. That is why it offers a second good model for the dynamics of shift.

Dialogue as I mean it here is not just any way of talking or discussing. It has its own distinctive rules, structure, and dynamic. Like any effective use of SQ, dialogue makes us surface and challenge the assumptions that support our motives. It leads to a change in our existing paradigms or mental models. It is a structure that dissolves previous structures.

The concept of dialogue began in the Athenian *agora* twenty-five hundred years ago and flowered with Socrates, but it then lay dormant in Western culture for centuries. In the 1940s, the practice was revived by group psychology as a new approach to group discussion and conflict resolution. In the 1970s, the quantum physicist David Bohm took up the cause of dialogue. He thought the process could change society. Through Bohm's work, dialogue began to spread. It was adopted by the MIT Learning Center and featured widely in Peter Senge's best-selling *The Fifth Discipline*. Bill Isaacs, a young protégé of Senge's, began the MIT Dialogue Project and took the practice into large companies. Today it is practiced widely, but its implications for bringing about SQ transformation and motivational change have not been articulated fully before.

In group psychology and in the corporate world, dialogue is practiced in what are called *dialogue groups*. Dialogue groups are also being run in schools, prisons, and local government offices. They've been used for conflict resolution in the Middle East and in western Asia. I personally have run them with companies, schools, and local politicians.

In the dialogue group, people sit in a circle to emphasize the lack of any hierarchy. A shop floor worker's voice has as much impact as that of the CEO. The ideal group size ranges from seven to twenty—large enough for diverse views, small enough so that everyone has an opportunity to participate fully. There can be no observers in the dialogue group, no fence-sitters. But one or preferably two members of the group also act as facilitators. They participate fully, they are members of the group, but they have the task of holding the group's energy and guiding the conversation gently to activate the twelve qualities of SQ. Many of those qualities are activated by the dialogue process itself—it does encourage *spontaneity*, develop *self-awareness*, cause members to *reframe* their paradigms, and incite *compassion*. Dialogue is by its nature a *celebration of diversity*, and so on.

The only real rules in dialogue are that each group member should express personal feelings and thoughts openly and honestly, and that no one should be abusive. Members must commit to attending the group regularly and vow to keep its conversation within the group itself. If the dialogue conversation should become too "clever" (cerebral), if there is abuse, or if the conversation collapses into confrontation, a facilitator gently brings it back on track.

The dialogue conversation acts as a powerful container for SQ transformation and behavioral shift because it has certain qualities that distinguish it from our normal way of discussing things. In these past two thousand years of Western culture, we've fallen into the habit of "debate," a peculiarly power-oriented, confrontational form of speech. As illustrated in Figure 8.3, debate is based on knowing and fighting for a personal position; dialogue is more about exploring the future and honoring the difference of many possible positions.

Good dialogue differs from debate in the following ways:

- *Finding out rather than knowing.* When I take part in a debate, I know what I am advocating or defending. I know my position is right. I participate in a debate with my head, with my IQ. Dialogue is about finding out (*asking Why?*),

Debate	Dialogue
Knowing	Finding out, discussion
Answers	Questions
Winning and losing	Sharing
Unequal	Equal
Power	Respect and reverence
Proving a point or defending a position	Exploring new possibilities and listening

Figure 8.3 *Debate versus Dialogue*

Note: Dialogue is *not* about reaching consensus.

about discussing something openly until I break through to some new knowledge or insight. I might go to a dialogue knowing what I *think* is the case, but I am willing to suspend my certainty and listen to the discussion with an open mind. And with an open heart. Dialogue involves my emotions and my deeper sensitivities as well as my best intellectual thinking faculties.

- *Questions rather than answers.* In debate, because I know, I have all the answers. I am here to teach you, or to convince you, or to defeat you. I talk *at* you. Dialogue is about questions (*asking Why?*), about the things I don't know (*humility*) or would like to find out. It's about exploration—of myself, of the others, of the matter at hand. Why do these words make me feel angry or anxious? Why have you said that? Where are you coming from? What is your point of view, and why do you hold it? Is that possibly another way to look at things? (*Reframing.*) What assumptions have I been harboring? Where has my point of view been coming from? What is my paradigm? (*Self-awareness.*)

- *Sharing rather than winning or losing.* In a debate, somebody knows, somebody has the answers, and the other person is wrong. One of us will win and the other will lose. One point of view will be judged better than the other, one line of argument best. Dialogue is about sharing (*compassion*). We share our points of view, we share our assumptions, our doubts and uncertainties, our questions, our fears and wild ideas, our *being*. We propose as many paths from A to B as we can jointly imagine and we consider them all together. We *feel* them together.

- *Equal rather than unequal.* Debate is unequal because one side is right and the other is wrong. One of us has the answers; the other is in error. One point of view will be judged better than the other. Someone will choose who has been more clever or more eloquent or more entertaining. Dialogue is equal because we all have something worthwhile to contribute (*celebration of diversity*). The vast majority of people have some valid reason for holding a point of view or harboring a feeling. There are no wrong points of view, no invalid ways to feel (*humility*). I am here to learn your reasons and your feelings and to understand their origins (*compassion*). And to understand my own response to them (*self-awareness*).

- *Respect or love rather than power.* Debate is about power. My power to defeat you or to persuade you or to make you compromise. My power to win you over or to make you look like a fool. Dialogue is about respect (*humility*). My respect for your point of view and how you have arrived at it, my respect for your feelings, your contribution. It may even be about love. My gratitude to you for seeing things differently than I do (*reframing*), my love for your different personality, your different history, your different experience, your ability to enrich me with them (*celebration of diversity*). Each of us can only live one of life's possibilities, and in dialogue we love those who can show us that other possibilities exist, love them for making those others possible.

- *Listening rather than proving a point.* Debate is about proving a point or defending a position. I attack you and I build defenses against you, against your point of view. I close myself to you, your words, and your feelings. I don't want to know. Most of us are not very good at listening. Our education and our experience have taught us to be ready with a thought or a reaction or a good argument. Conversation is a game of Ping Pong. This overpreparedness blocks out what we might learn or hear or become. It makes us insensitive—to others and to ourselves. Dialogue is about exploring new possibilities. It is about listening. I create a space inside myself where I can hear you, where I can feel what you are saying. I create a space inside myself where I can hear myself (*self-awareness*), where I can listen to and feel my own reactions to what you say (*spontaneity*).

Dialogue groups are powerful vehicles for deep motivational and behavioral change. They embed the main principles of SQ and they encourage us to relate to ourselves, each other, and our work from a place of higher motivation. They instill vision and values and, at their best, create leaders who act from +5, *creativity,* or even +6, *higher service* (servant leaders, or knights). A good dialogue group is an enriching and creative experience. A great one is almost a sacred rite.

To me, dialogue is essentially an *attitude.* It is a radically different attitude toward oneself, toward others, toward knowledge and problems and relationships. It is a new paradigm, SQ in practice, and an important tool for building the kind of culture required for spiritual capital to flourish. If, deep inside ourselves and in our approach to others, we replaced knowing with finding out, answers with questions, winning or losing with sharing, power with respect and love, and proving points with exploring possibilities and listening, then I think we really could change ourselves and our world. We would certainly see a different approach to work, innovation, challenge, and relationship. The deep purposes of our corporations and business lives would alter and broaden, making the building of spiritual capital possible.

The Right Conditions for Shift

I have already pointed out that motivational, and thus cultural, shift happens most readily in times of crisis, when our existing way of going about things has not worked and we or our organization are in a period of instability. But the possibility, or indeed the direction, of shift is also influenced by the attitude with which we go about it. An attitude of control or manipulation can block or distort the SQ energies that might bear on the motivations underlying the crisis. Those who want to grow or change for the wrong reasons may well end up more stunted.

I knew a business consultant in South Africa who feared (−4, *fear*) that he lacked power with people. His wife agreed with him, and indeed nagged him that their marriage would improve if he showed more power with her. She thought he would make more money if he could show more power with his clients. To please his wife and to impress his clients, he decided to join Aikido classes. This is a martial arts technique that teaches participants to find their own physical center of gravity (in the abdomen), and to act from there. They should acquire +3, *power-within*. But this consultant's motive for taking up Aikido was −3, *craving*, a craving to please his wife and to impress his clients. And he thought he could overcome his lack of power by sheer self-assertion, through learning a technique. After a year of attending, the Aikido classes had done him no good. Indeed, he now felt some *anguish* (−5) because his efforts had failed.

It is impossible to raise a low motive to a higher one without some help, either, as noted in Chapter Three, through the beneficial influence or example of a leader or a culture, or through opening ourselves to the energies of SQ transformation. In both, the operative word is *openness*. It is impossible to ride with the creativity of a complex adaptive system by trying to control it. It is impossible to make a significant shift in attitude, behavior, and outlook without a certain surrender to forces (or something or someone) larger than ourselves. In Christianity, this is known as surrendering to grace; in Buddhism, the surrender of craving; and in Taoism a surrender to the forces of the universe, the *Tao*, The Way. Jesus, on committing his life to higher service, said, "Not my will, Lord, but thine." In Alcoholics Anonymous, they say, "Let Go. Let God." Great motivational shift is a deeply spiritual process. Through it our deepest meanings and values shift, our deepest purposes alter. We come into possession of a new life (or organizational) strategy. A shift of such magnitude is beyond the unaided power of the human ego.

Five Steps to Shift

- Know that shift is possible. No one ever has to be stuck.
- See where you are now, and thoroughly analyze its causes and consequences.
- *Want* to shift, and be prepared to let go.
- See where you want to get to.
- Nurture the relevant qualities of SQ, or all of them.

Shifting Corporate Culture

For the vast majority of people, the wider culture in which they operate is like the sea in which a fish might swim. The seawater is taken into the fish through its gills and permeates all its cells. It is impossible to draw any firm boundary between where sea ends and fish begins. As Arthur Miller once observed, "The fish is in the sea, and the sea is in the fish." For us, then, that "sea" is the shared field of meaning in which our consciousness is immersed, and that shared field is our culture. Culture contains our shared motives, our common behavior, our joint attitudes. It contains patterns of meaning and common values. Unless we stand back and reflect on it, the impact that culture has on us as individuals is largely subconscious.

We humans and our relationship to culture are much more complex than fish and seawater. For us, there are many cultures that impinge on us (permeate us), and many different levels of our behavior are influenced. Each of us is immersed in a strong family culture with its own dominant and recurring behavior patterns.

Many of us never outgrow this family culture, and we carry it with us throughout life in our intimate and social relationships. We are also immersed in the wider cultures of the various groups to which we belong, including our national or ethnic culture and the culture of our workplace. If these various cultures are stuck in low motivations and self-destructive behavior, they tend to drag us down. By contrast, a culture driven by more positive motivations and their accompanying ideals and values can inspire us as individuals and raise the levels of our own behavior and attitudes. Shifting culture, where that culture is negative, is critical to our human well-being. Here, we are most concerned with how to shift business culture, but the work we do on this will have broad implications for behavioral shift in other dimensions of our lives. Education, politics, and broadcasting are obvious examples.

Though for most people culture is a dominant influence, and shifting it the desired goal that will affect the greatest number of individuals, the task of that shift itself must begin with at least a critical mass of individuals. Some of us must make the culture rather than letting the culture make us. In the business world, the task of shifting culture will fall to a critical mass of enlightened leaders and the infrastructures they can create for enabling shift. These infrastructures will include the methods, style, and content of human resources programs and perhaps the intervention of consultants. The goal is to create a whole new field of meaning from which the majority of individuals can draw in attempting to shift their own behavior.

It is nothing new to say that a business culture must change if we want to bring about behavioral change. Many consultants specialize in attempting just this. But most transformation programs start from the wrong end, and they act from too narrow a perspective. They aspire too low and work at the shallow end of motivation theory. If the underlying motivation of a transformation program itself is to sustain the old paradigm, the attitudes and ethos of profit-dominated business-as-usual, the resulting "transformation" will not bring about lasting or meaningful shift. It is, as I described in my earlier book, *Rewiring the Corporate Brain,* equivalent to just shifting some furniture about in an existing room. The place looks different for a while, but in the end we just have the same old furniture and the same old room. Even those transformation programs that would bring in some new furniture, that is, some genuinely new patterns of working, or even aspire to some different results do not focus on the level where real shift happens. If we want to do that, we have to blow up the structures of the room itself. That means shifting underlying *motives,* by shifting the values that underlie them. We don't *begin* by trying to shift the culture.

The dynamic of lasting shift, if approached from the right direction, begins, then, with shifting motives through bringing to bear the forces of SQ. But because motives are what drive behavior, a shift in motives leads to a consequent shift in behavior. In turn, it is our behavior that creates and then reflects our culture. It is only when we have brought about significant *behavioral* shift that we can then go on to expect and enable a *cultural* shift. The dynamic of lasting shift is from motivational shift to behavioral shift to cultural shift, as summarized in Figure 9.1. Organizational infrastructures will then evolve that can enable and preserve the shift. If organizational transformers want to shift culture, they must begin at the beginning.

In the case of the British steel mill described in Chapter Eight, where quite substantial cultural shift was realized in the end, the first stages of shift concentrated

Figure 9.1 *Organizational Shift Dynamics: A Feedback Loop*

on raising the motivations of a critical mass of the leadership and workforce. It was only when motivations had shifted from *self-assertion* (−1), *anger* (−2), *craving* (−3), and *fear* (−4) to *exploration* (+1), *cooperation* (+2), *power-within* (+3), and *mastery* (+4) that a noticeable shift in behavior could then show itself in a cultural shift.

Behavioral Indicators of Shift

I have discussed individual motivational shift and its dynamics in some depth in preceding chapters. But it is difficult to measure or detect that shift until it gets expressed by a shift in behavior and attitudes. That is, we can't see a person's motives (though we can have an intuition of them), but we *can* describe and categorize their behavior.

Given patterns of behavior that correlate with the twelve processes of SQ, it is possible to describe the kind of behavior that *indicates* high SQ, and thus higher motivation. This is the kind of behavior we would hope to see, at grassroots level, that could lead to a high-SQ culture.

In the following paragraphs I describe the kind of behavior that would indicate the processes of SQ at work, drawing on behavioral and cultural indicators of high SQ that were devised largely by Peter Saul. This is, as I say, hands-on behavior at the grassroots level, the kind of behavior we would need to employ on a daily basis in the workplace for there to be the chance of a consequent cultural shift toward higher motivations.

Self-Awareness
- Encourages people to ask for feedback from others on their decisions and performance
- Has a sense of long-term goals and strategies
- Anticipates the impact of personal actions on others
- Assesses personal strengths and weaknesses in line with how others see them
- Has a deep sense of what this organization is "about"—its ideals, its values, its deep purpose and direction

Vision and Value Led
- Seeks to know how the work can make a real difference to customers and clients, the community, the less-well-off, and so on
- Expresses concern when the organization fails to live by its stated values
- Makes career choices guided by a desire to do something worthwhile with life
- Is prepared to fight for matters of principle

- Argues for performance measures that go beyond financial or operational numbers to include environmental and social impacts

Positive Use of Adversity

- Seeks to learn from mistakes rather than blaming others for them
- Is prepared to tackle challenging tasks despite a risk of failure
- Persists with a task in the face of difficulties
- Draws on hidden reserves of energy and motivation when things go wrong
- Can usually see a bright side to difficult situations

Holistic

- Encourages people to understand the operation of the whole organization
- Anticipates the longer-term consequences of today's actions and decisions
- Seeks to balance working and nonworking life
- Involves others who will be affected by the outcome when planning and making decisions
- Is creative in using ideas drawn from fields outside the current work or profession to solve work problems or improve performance

Compassion

- Expresses concern for the welfare of others
- Considers the way external stakeholders will feel about actions or decisions the organization might take
- Is sensitive to the feeling and needs of other people in the workplace

- Tries to ensure the organization has a positive impact on the natural and social environments
- Is willing to make the time to help others

Celebration of Diversity

- Does as much as possible to ensure a wide and heterogeneous mix of employees
- Seeks input from a wide range of people when planning or making decisions
- Respects and seriously considers ideas that challenge the mainstream
- Encourages people to express their individuality at work
- Explores a range of possible options before making decisions

Field Independence

- Is prepared to fight for a personal point of view when sure of its correctness
- Is prepared to make unpopular decisions when necessary for the good of the team or organization
- Listens to the views of others, but is always prepared to take responsibility for personal decisions and actions
- Is not easily swayed by the popular or majority opinion
- Is not easily distracted when involved in an important task

Tendency to Ask Fundamental Why Questions

- Makes sure to understand the causes of problems before initiating corrective action
- Looks for patterns behind problems or failures and seeks to understand their origin or meaning

- Seeks to understand the factors that lead to high or low performance in the field
- Gives others opportunities to explain their actions before giving negative feedback
- Encourages people to question company policies and procedures when they think performance is inhibited or could be improved

Reframing
- Brings a variety of approaches to problem-solving tasks
- Is prepared to let go of previously held ideas and past decisions when these clearly are not working
- Is good at seeing the big picture—the wider context, the longer view
- Often comes up with unusual or out-in-left-field ideas and suggestions for improving things at work
- Seeks to broaden experience by taking on tasks and assignments outside the comfort zone

Spontaneity
- Is prepared to experiment and take risks in order to enhance performance
- Is prepared to back a hunch or gut feeling about what will add value at work
- Is prepared to change a plan or agenda to meet changing circumstances or to pursue an exciting opportunity
- Actively seeks opportunities to have fun at work
- Seeks to foster creativity by encouraging others to explore seemingly crazy ideas

A Sense of Vocation
- Goes that extra mile to achieve an excellent result

- Shows deep interest in and satisfaction with the work
- Sees work as an important part of life
- Expresses appreciation for the opportunities and gifts received at home and at work
- Encourages the organization to be socially responsible

Humility
- Looks to give others credit for their knowledge and achievements
- Defers to the greater knowledge or experience of others
- Recognizes being part of a team and that other members' views are important too
- Is prepared to explore what can be learned from personal mistakes
- Seeks to bring others on board by being open to their suggestions and deep concerns

These behavioral indicators of high SQ point clearly to the kind of behavior and attendant attitudes of openness and mutual respect that most of us would like to see in our place of work. Indeed, they would create a good atmosphere for cooperation and learning in any group situation, from the family to the smooth operation of a democratic government or an educational system that brings out the best qualities and potential in children. A great deal of work-related stress would diminish if they were widely distributed, and people would be more positively involved in their work. But what kind of attendant cultural shift would embed these qualities in group attitudes (groupwide higher motivation) that can reach back and draw in the majority of the management structure and workforce of an organization or institution (the feedback loop in Figure 9.1)? Where are the active "pressure points" in an organizational culture where we should look to focus such a shift?

Eight Issues That Focus Organizational Culture

In my own work with and observation of organizational cultures, eight issues seem to crop up again and again as topics that concern people. These eight issues focus the energy and interactions of people within the organization and are thus the areas of culture on which to focus shift. All have a direct effect on how smoothly individuals in the organization work as a corporate whole, and thus a consequent effect on productivity, including its low-stress component. If high-SQ behavior could dominate in these eight areas, I believe that a high-SQ (higher-motivation) culture would emerge. Such a high-SQ culture is the bedrock of any paradigm shift from business-as-usual to the overarching vision I have been calling spiritual capital (a values-based capitalism). As shown in Figure 9.2, the eight issues are communication, fairness, relationships, trust, power, truth, flexibility, and empowerment.

Communication	Fairness
Relationships	Trust
Power	Truth
Flexibility	Empowerment

Figure 9.2 *Eight Key Issues for Corporate Culture*

In most organizations, communication is not what it could be. On one hand employees complain of being deluged (usually by e-mail) with an overwhelming amount of useless information; on the other they feel they do not really know what those in power are thinking and planning, especially as it affects them. Communication between different departments, divisions, and sectors is usually poor, thus interfering with the emergence of a holistic culture where employees can see the patterns and connections at work in their organization as a whole.

The amount of fairness (or its lack) perceived to exist in an organization has a direct effect on morale and on the likelihood that employees will give their all or grudgingly stick to what is required. It also affects teamwork and relationships in general. Relationships, trust, and truth cannot be separated—each impinges on the others. We need to trust that others will tell us the truth, however unpalatable, and we need to trust that they will stand by us in times of crisis or if we should make mistakes when taking a risk on behalf of the organization. Power permeates any organization. It is necessary to any organization, but how is it wielded? Is it perceived to be fair? Is it shared among a wide range of people? Does it lead to empowerment of individuals? Are the dictates of power themselves flexible, and does the organization's power structure lead to easy flexibility in methodology and decision making?

The negative culture surrounding these eight issues in business-as-usual accounts for the fact that at least 85 percent of the people in the workforce are influenced to act from the negative motivations of −1, −2, −3, and −4. And that in turn accounts for why business itself is driven by a culture expressing *self-assertion, anger, craving,* and *fear.* The feedback loop effect again! Business-as-we-know-it is caught in a vicious and unsustainable circle of negative motivation.

To break out of this vicious circle, a critical mass of senior management in any organization must shift to more positive, higher-SQ behavior with respect to the eight issues that dominate business culture. The next task is to focus on what form that positive behavior might take to have the power to shift cultural attitudes and infrastructures.

Indicators of Shift to a Culture That Fosters High SQ

In this section, I return to grassroots behavior, to positive expressions of each of the eight cultural issues as they might be experienced by any employee of an organization—the "I" who speaks in each statement. In this case, each of the eight issues has itself been correlated with the twelve processes of SQ, to highlight the salient features of a culture that exhibits high SQ and thus is a culture that encourages action from higher motivations.

Communication
- Senior management ensures that all employees know and understand the organization's goals, vision, and strategy.
- Managers make sure that I know how my job contributes to the achievement.
- Early reporting of bad news or potential threats to organizational performance is encouraged in this company.
- People get timely and accurate feedback on their performance.

- Staff are encouraged to seek regular feedback from their internal and external customers or clients on how they can better meet their needs.
- All employees are given opportunity to contribute in a meaningful way to decisions affecting them.

Fairness

- The workload is distributed fairly among members of my team.
- I am rewarded fairly for my knowledge, skills, and contribution to this organization.
- Appointments and promotions in this organization go to the person who is best suited to a job.
- People are helped to learn from honest mistakes, rather than being punished.
- The company supports people when pressures from family or personal life negatively affect their performance.
- Managers respect ideas and suggestions put forward by all members of a unit or team.

Relationships

- Senior managers care about the well-being of people who work here.
- Some of the people I work with have become good friends.
- The organization strives to develop mutually beneficial, long-term relationships with its stakeholders (customers, shareholders, business partners, community, and environmental groups).
- When plans and budgets are made in this organization, the people issues that we will need

to consider in reaching our goals are carefully considered.

- My manager helps me to arrange my working hours and conditions so there is a minimum of stress on my relationships outside work.
- People in different departments or sectors of this organization cooperate to achieve common goals.

Trust

- The level of trust between managers and workers in this organization is high.
- Important information about the health of the business is shared freely with all employees.
- I can rely on other people I work with to do their jobs well.
- My manager backs me when I make a decision about my job.
- Other members of my team help me out when I am overloaded or have problems in my job.
- I feel safe in experimenting and taking reasonable risks in order to maximize my performance.

Power

- Senior managers do not have a lot more privileges than lower-level staff.
- Senior managers do not bend the rules to suit themselves in this organization.
- Senior managers provide adequate opportunities for me to speak with them about how I believe things are going in this organization.
- I am not afraid of the power that senior management has over me.
- Senior managers listen to my ideas or suggestions for improvement instead of just telling me what to do.

- I feel this organization uses its power to further the common good of stakeholders.

Truth

- I can believe the information that senior management gives me.
- I am encouraged to give managers honest and timely feedback on any matter affecting current performance or the future success of the organization.
- When changes are planned in this organization, the likely impact is fully discussed with people to be affected by them.
- There are few hidden agendas in this organization.
- The public documents published by this organization give stakeholders a true and complete account of its performance and intentions.
- I am encouraged to tell the truth in my job.

Flexibility

- I have considerable scope to tailor my arrangements to my preferred way of working.
- When changes in the external environment make it impossible to achieve agreed performance targets, I can discuss the matter with my manager and suggest changes to the original plan.
- We anticipate likely trends and events that may affect our performance and develop contingency plans to deal with them.
- People are encouraged to acquire a range of skills so they can contribute to the organization in a variety of ways.

- Our management processes and our technology allow us great flexibility on the job.
- We try to enable our customers to do business with us in a way that suits them best.

Empowerment
- I feel able to influence the organization's plans and policies that affect me and my work.
- I have plenty of scope to use initiative in my job.
- I have been delegated enough authority to do my job well.
- When I make a mistake in my work, it is left to me to initiate corrective action.
- This organization invests in the continuing development of my knowledge and skills.
- We listen to feedback from our customers (internal and external) and stakeholders and act on it to improve performance.

An organizational culture that exhibits the characteristics outlined in this section is the goal. If we could bring about that extent of cultural shift in a business (or any other organization), we would be well on our way to having created a high-SQ culture that can focus on amassing spiritual capital. But the goal still needs means to attain it. Throughout this book, and particularly in the last few chapters, I have stressed the necessity of creating a critical mass of leadership elite who are themselves moved by higher motivations. This critical mass can then work an atmosphere of higher motivation throughout the organization and into its culture. In the next chapter, I will look in some depth at the creation and discovery of this leadership elite.

10

A New Knights Templar?

This new order of knights is one that is unknown by the ages. They fight two wars, one against the adversaries of flesh and blood, and another against a spiritual army of wickedness in the heavens. . . . Truly they are fearless knights and completely secure. While their bodies are properly armed for these circumstances, their souls are also clothed with the armor of faith. On all sides surely they are well armed; they fear neither demons nor men.

—St. Bernard of Clairvaux, on the Knights Templar

The Knights Templar of the early Middle Ages were soldier monks of the Christian Church who rode into battle to serve their god.[1] They were excellent soldiers who practiced all the martial arts of knighthood, but they also prepared themselves for battle with meditation (prayer), with self-sacrifice, with service, and by taking holy vows. All knights of the Middle Ages followed a code of chivalry, but the Templars had a further, sacred dedication. Unlike the "worldly knights," who fought for wealth, honor, and glory, and who dressed themselves in the most magnificent regalia, the Templars took vows of personal poverty, modesty, and chastity. Their warrior costume was a simple white cloak emblazoned with a red cross.

The Templars were founded to protect Christian pilgrims visiting the Holy Land. But their wider vision was to "recapture Jerusalem"—a powerful metaphor for recapturing or for building all that is best on earth. This is a metaphor used also by Jews and Muslims, both of whom also look to Jerusalem as their spiritual center. Every action the Templar knights took, every battle they fought, was inspired by their holy commitment to serving life's deeper dimensions. In the process, their order amassed great wealth. Bearing in mind today's ever-present obsession with the bottom line, it is relevant to know that the Knights Templar were, in material terms, the richest monastic order in all Christendom. Their idealism, reputation, and wealth were too much for the greed of the French king and the power-hungry rulers of the Roman Catholic Church, who exterminated the order en masse through a joint conspiracy. The Knights' service and their legend have lived on through their influence on the later Grail legends, on the crafts guilds of the later Middle Ages, and particularly through the early dedication and esoteric teachings of the Order of Freemasons. The contemporary Masonic movement survives as little more than a social club, but Masonic scholars insist that the spirit, teachings, and rituals of the Templars are still there to be found in the literature and lesser-known practices of the Masons.[2] Over the centuries, of course, some quite unpleasant movements have also seen themselves as inspired by the Knights Templar. The most recent known to me was Heinrich Himmler's evocation of the Templars to support Nazi mythology. I abhor such misuse of the Templar legend and trust that it will not color the reception of my discussion here.

It is not the Christianity nor even the specific esoteric doctrines of the Knights Templar that makes me tell their story here. There have been similar holy warriors in other cultures—the Assassins of Islam, the Japanese Samurai, and the Chinese Shao-Lin Kung Fu masters among them. I highlight the Templars because, in the Western tradition, they are the most potent example of a worldly efficacy combined with a deep spiritual dedication. Their specific dedication to the Christian cross is less important than the broader fact that they dedicated their worldly lives to the service of that which they held most sacred. This is why I believe their story can be an inspiring model for contemporary business (and other) leaders who would dedicate themselves to changing the culture of capitalism and business from within. The word knight itself derives from the Old English word *cniht,* which means "a servant." The modern Templars are today's "servant leaders," the men or women who serve their most fundamental values and purposes through doing more highly motivated work in the world. These are the men and women who are needed to build spiritual capital for our organizations. It is they who will lead the way in building sustainable capitalism.

The great nineteenth-century American philanthropists, the Quaker businessmen, and some other capitalists of Victorian England were driven by the spirit of the Knights Templar. In the few places where that spirit can be found today, it is usually in the public sector or among the global aid agencies. But I have had the good fortune to know some contemporary executives who strive and serve in the Templar spirit. They are men and women who want their business lives to "make a difference," and who in both their business and personal lives are driven by high ideals and deep concern. They, and others like them, demonstrate that some significant shift in business culture toward the ideal of spiritual capital is not unrealistic. I have already written about Mats Lederhausen from McDonald's. Here I would like to tell the inspirational story of Michael Rennie, a partner of McKinsey & Co. based in Sydney.

The Making of a Knight

Michael Rennie was, as he says of himself, "the golden boy." He still has curly golden hair and an open, boyish face that defies the imprint of age. Very bright as a youth, he traveled on a Rhodes Scholarship from his native Perth to Oxford University, where he studied philosophy, languages, and economics. After a further degree in law, he returned to Australia and joined the ranks of McKinsey. "I had it all," says Michael. "I loved the game, and I loved the material advantages of my life. I was good at what I did." Then, suddenly, at the age of thirty-one, Michael was told that he had only six months to live. He had been diagnosed with Hodgkin's disease, a cancer that destroys the body's white blood cells. Miraculously, he is still alive today to tell the story, at the age of forty-three.

"I did all the usual chemotherapy treatment that the hospital required," he says, "but I also looked elsewhere." In fact, Michael put himself largely in the hands of an alternative therapist who taught him meditation and positive thinking techniques. He became convinced of the mind's power to regenerate white blood cells. "I don't know for certain what it was," he says now, "but my cancer went into remission, and here I am today." But the Michael who is here today is not quite the same Michael who was diagnosed twelve years ago.

"For a long time, anyway," he says, "there had been two people within me. One was the person who loved the excitement and the stimulation of the material world. And there was another part that was becoming increasingly reflective. My friends joked that I would either run the country or go to Nimbin [the center of Australia's counterculture]. . . . There was a struggle between the two me's; they weren't integrated and for a long time I thought it was a choice. . . . After the cancer I came to realize that it wasn't a choice: it was about integration, and I came to know that if I didn't integrate the two, I would get sick again."

Back at McKinsey now as a partner, Michael devotes much of his time and most of his creative energy to his new "cultural capital" leadership program, which views values, spirit, and meaning as being as important as cost-containment, corporate strategy, and the bottom line. When I last saw him six months ago, he was taking the top two thousand executives of an Australian bank through a three-day program aimed, he says, at boosting their spiritual intelligence. He calls the focus of his work "cultural capital," but I believe he means by that everything that I mean by "spiritual capital." He wants to change business culture, and through it wider society, to being more focused on fundamental human values and more widely serving human purposes.

"Business," he says, "is the most powerful institution on earth today. It is more powerful than politics. Business serves us very well in some ways, but it doesn't serve us as fully as it should; it doesn't serve us fully as people." Toward achieving that wider end, Michael is devoting his life's work to creating a new caste of business leaders. He is doing so by drawing on his own wider vision, values, and a life's passion won by confronting death.

In fact, the 5 percent of Western people who have had near-death experiences are often changed by this, the ultimate "edge of chaos" situation any of us can know.[3]

Michael Rennie is an example par excellence of the kind of business leader I hold up as a prototype for a new order of knights inspired by the Knights Templar. Like the Templar model, he excels in worldly, business street-wisdom. He knows the game and how to play it. At the same time, since his battle with cancer, he is dedicated to a higher service and he can use that dedication effectively, *plus* his street-wisdom, to inspire and train others. That combination of head and heart, usually won through some great crisis or life-changing event, is one of the most salient qualities of a "knight." It provides the capacity and the credentials to lead others toward the higher motivation needed to transform culture. Knights are the leadership elite we need to amass spiritual capital in our business culture.

The Qualities of a Knight

Worldly business expertise plus an overarching vision or drive to serve higher values define the essential quality of a knight. But there is more. If knights are to lead others and to inspire others toward higher motivation, they must themselves be grounded in something deeper, something more transpersonal, than the culture that surrounds them. They must be in a position, as I said earlier, to make their culture rather than to be made by it. They are the true "movers and shakers" from Arthur O'Shaughnessy's famous "Ode": "We are the music-makers,/ And we are the dreamers of dreams,/ . . . Yet we are the movers and shakers/ Of the world for ever, it seems." Located at +6, *higher service,* on the Scale of Motivations, knights are made by their values. Those values are their access to the transpersonal.

Knights are made, not born. They are made by their experience and by the way they respond to that experience. Being told that he would die in six months might have led Michael Rennie to despair. In that case, he would be an example for no one and he would probably be dead. Instead, he responded with the SQ quality *positive use of adversity* and acquired the *sense of vocation* that led to +6, *higher service.* But I know through speaking with him that it was a long and arduous journey. He says himself that he had to strip himself down to get to his most fundamental values. He had to reflect on those "deep questions" like the meaning of life, the meaning of *his* life, his most fundamental purposes. And all that in turn meant stripping himself of less deep values, of self-deception, and of unconscious assumptions. It is almost a process of being reborn. Michael now uses this "stripping down" process on the executives he takes through his leadership program, getting them, as a first step toward transformation, to peel themselves back to basics. The next and crucial step is to find a way to *live* the fundamental values that we find at the core of ourselves. That is what leads to the knight's *sense of vocation.*

Most of us are fortunate enough not to be confronted with the possibility of early and imminent death. But we do confront other crises that give us the opportunity to change ourselves. Many lose loved ones, lose their families through divorce, go through bankruptcy, lose their jobs, suffer serious injury or illness, or simply wake up one morning not liking themselves or their lives very much. Many others just feel a vague discontent, or a tiredness of life. All such crises can lead to despair or apathy, but they have the potential to lead to rebirth and self-renewal. The deciding factor is having the spiritual guts to access the "deep self" and the fundamental values latent within it. Most will need some help—the spiritual companionship of a wise friend, a spiritual mentor, wide reading, a well-run transformation program. Michael Rennie sought the help of a meditation master.

I spoke at some length earlier of the importance of self-organizing systems poised at the edge of chaos. Being poised between order and chaos, between the known and the unknown, is what gives these systems their unfolding creativity. Knights, if you like, are "souls at the edge," leaders poised at the edge between the world as it is and the world as it could be. They have learned to live with terror, with uncertainty and with ambiguity, anchored always in their fundamental values. The knights of old were distinguished by bravery and valor in battle. They risked their lives for their faith. The knights I envision today risk *themselves.* They live life as an unfolding experiment, trusting that that experiment has a direction and purpose of its own that they serve.

The German philosopher Friedrich Nietzsche spoke of the difference between leadership (commanding) and obedience in these terms: "Commanding is more difficult than obeying. And not only because the commander bears the burden of all who obey, and that this burden can easily crush him. But in all commanding there appeared to me an experiment and a risk; and the living creature always risks himself when he commands."[4]

The Credo of a Knight

Knights are leaders embarked on a spiritual path. Through personal experience they have gained a sense of something fundamentally sacred underlying human life. This may have no adequate human name, symbol, or description. This sense of the sacred is at the core of all living religions and spiritual experiences, but it is not fully encompassed by any one of them. It has variously been called God, Lord, the Creator, the Source, the Deep Self, Being, the Void, or the quantum vacuum. By whatever name they give it, it is the source of the knights' ultimate identities, meanings, and concerns. It is what they wish to embed in their actions and in their life's work.

In both life and work, the knight abides by five principles:

- There is something sacred, some deeper, shared consciousness, unfolding in this universe and providing a baseline for every aspect of life.
- Life and all its enterprises are interconnected.
- All human endeavor, including business, is part of the larger and richer fabric of the whole universe.
- The relationship of the healthy individual to the world is one of engagement and responsibility.

- Service conveys deep sense of humility and gratitude.

These five principles, I believe, are incorporated within what we could call the Credo of a Knight. I have written the credo of a business knight in the accompanying sidebar. Knights in other fields can use it as a model to write their own.

Knights, as I have defined them, are high in spiritual intelligence and both possess and create great spiritual capital—the amount of spiritual awareness and expertise available to them or their organizations. They therefore possess in large measure the SQ quality of *celebrating diversity*. This means their credo is held more deeply than the beliefs of any specific religion or culture, that it transcends any difference in gender or race, and that it excludes the access of no one on such grounds.

The Credo of a Business Knight

I believe that global business has the money and the power to make a significant difference in today's troubled world, and that by making that difference it can help itself as well as others. I envision business raising its sights above the bottom line. I envisage business becoming a vocation, like the higher professions. To make this possible I believe that business must add a moral dimension, becoming more service- and value-oriented and largely eliminating the assumed natural distinction between private enterprise and public institutions. I envisage business taking responsibility for the world in which it operates and from which it creates its wealth. And I envisage myself becoming one of those business leaders who are "servant leaders"—leaders who serve not just stockholders, colleagues, employees, products, and customers, but leaders who also serve the community, the planet, humanity, the future, and life itself.

What, then, is the purpose of the knight (or servant leader), and what is the path that the knight follows? In the words of the great Hindu mystic Ramana Maharshi, "It is to learn the truth that all one's actions performed with unselfish devotion, with the aid of the purified mind, body and speech, in the capacity of the servant of the Lord, become the Lord's actions, and to stand free from the sense of 'I' and 'mine.' This is also the truth of what is called supreme devotion, or living in the service of God."[5]

In the Christian tradition, the Order of Trappist monks have as their motto the words, *Laborare est orare,* "to work is to pray." For the knights, their work is their prayer. Their lives are a way of being embedded in a way of doing.

Knights and Masters

Knights are motivated by +6, *higher service.* Masters are motivated by +4, *mastery.* Knights work to *change* the paradigm and then introduce that new paradigm into the culture through their service. Masters work *within* a paradigm and are the masters of their existing paradigm. But masters are also open to the creative input of knights, and it is they who embed the knights' new vision within actual infrastructures and relationships in an organization. Knights bring an input of spiritual capital. Masters use this new spiritual capital to build their organizations' social capital.

In the corporate world (or politics), masters are found at the level of really good CEOs or government ministers. In schools, masters are likely to be head teachers. They know their tradition and how to perpetuate it and how to bring out its best potential. Knights

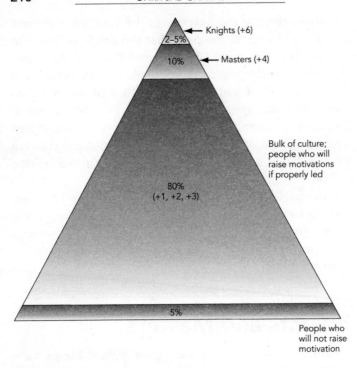

Knights (+6)

Masters (+4)

2–5%

10%

Bulk of culture;
people who will
raise motivations
if properly led

80%
(+1, +2, +3)

5%

People who
will not raise
motivation

Figure 10.1　*Motivational Pyramid After Cultural Shift*

will most likely be recruited from the ranks of masters.
Their knightly task is then to move on to +5, *creativity,*
and +6, *higher service.* For this, the would-be knights
may need gurus or higher masters to help them, people
to whom the knight can become a pupil or apprentice.
This is the highest level of mentoring possible within a
corporate setting. Knights, in turn, can mentor masters
to bring out their best qualities of mastery.

How Many Knights Are Needed?

It is a well-known sociological law that a 10 percent minority in any culture begins to unsettle and change that culture. But 10 percent knights seems too optimistic. I would argue that if the leadership of an organization can contain 2–5 percent knights (paradigm-shifting servant leaders), and a further 10 percent masters, that culture will have a leadership profile sufficient to raise the motivation level of the whole organization from *fear* (−4), *craving* (−3), *anger* (−2), and *self-assertion* (−1) into the positive motivational zone of *exploration* (+1), *cooperation* (+2), and *power-within* (+3). A shift of this dimension would be sufficient to move the culture into one that possesses a significant degree of spiritual capital.

To give a profile of an organization that can produce and embed spiritual capital, I offer the sketch in Figure 10.1, which depicts an organizational change model originally presented by R.M. Moorthy of Motorola University. I have adapted it for my purposes here. The logic of the model is that if the top 5 percent of an organization are knights, and the next 10 percent masters, then a further 80 percent of the organizational culture will be led to raise their own motivations. In Moorthy's model, there is always 5 percent at the bottom who never change.

Is It Still Capitalism?

I have argued throughout this book that spiritual capital is a vital component of sustainable capitalism, and of the sustainability of individuals and organizations functioning within an open, capitalist society. That has been the *raison d'être* of the book, showing individuals how they can access, draw on, and embed their deepest meanings and values in their lives, families, communities, and organizations to ensure sustainability. But as capitalism traditionally has been value neutral and without a moral dimension, skeptics might wonder whether it would still be capitalism if we added these. Wouldn't embedding deep values and exercising moral concern for wider society constrain the freedom and flexibility so vital to the very essence of capitalism and an open society?

Past attempts to control, constrain, or replace capitalism, all motivated by a desire to limit its wider excesses and to make it more socially responsible, have not offered encouraging results. Marxism, socialism, Keynesianism, and Europe's new Third Way have all failed to match the dynamism and material wealth-creating abilities of free-market capitalism. Their accompanying social ideals have in some cases limited the individual and institutional freedoms necessary to an open society. But there is a very sound, single reason for these failures, the same in each case. They failed to understand the kind of system that an open capitalist society and economy is (they failed to understand its essential dynamics), and their remedial measures had the unavoidable effect of further damaging the patient. They could not have done otherwise.

As noted earlier, an open, capitalist society, one that is sustainable and able to maintain itself and evolve into the future, is a special kind of entity that scientists call a *complex adaptive system,* or a self-organizing complex system. All living systems are such systems, including ourselves and our sustainable organizations. It is vital to the definition of such systems that matter and energy and information flow freely through them, that they are organized *from the inside,* and that they are poised at the edge of chaos—at a critical point far from equilibrium.

Many familiar systems in nature are such systems—the weather, our planet's ecosystem, anthills, beehives, our own bodies and brains. Complexity scientists have now included such systems as stock markets, free market economies, and open societies.[1] All such systems are dampened down or crushed by outside attempts to control them or to make them more stable. They lose their dynamism and their creativity. It is like putting a man or woman in a straitjacket or subjecting someone to brainwashing and then demanding a free expression of belief. All past attempts to make capitalism more socially responsible were the equivalent of straitjackets, *imposing control from the outside.*

By contrast, arguing that spiritual capital is vital to sustainable capitalism is based on saying that an input of values and conscience is a necessary ingredient of a human sustainable system's own *self-organizing* capacities. These are not values or conscience dictated by somebody else. They are the deeply transpersonal values and moral principles of the people who live and work within such systems. I am saying that such a system cannot maintain itself and evolve into the future without this input. But this input of spiritual capital that adds to the system's self-organizing capacity is *essentially* different from any kind of outside control. It is a different paradigm, embodying different attitudes, assumptions, and action plans.

Making it clear why this is so will enable me to sum up and tie together the main theme and sub-themes that have run through the book. It will become clear what the dynamics of a human self-organizing complex system are, why these require spiritual intelligence to give an input of spiritual capital, why knights and masters play such a vital role, and why spiritual capital is vital to the sustainability of individuals, organizations, and an open capitalist society.

Dynamics of a Human Complex Adaptive System

Natural and living systems can exist in one of four states: closed systems, steady-state systems, complex adaptive systems, and turbulence (chaos). In their human equivalents, the first three of these states all require that the system has material capital (raw materials), social capital (relationships, community customs, and institutions), and spiritual capital (meaning, values, purpose). No human system can be sustainable without all three kinds of capital.

A closed system is essentially like one of those large glass vases filled with plants and topped with a cork. The earth, original moisture and nutrients from the soil, the oxygen and carbon dioxide trapped in the air, and light passing through the vase, allow a self-sustaining photosynthesis for at least a season's life cycle. A pond in a field is another such system, though slightly more complex because it may maintain a symbiotic balance between plants and some fish, between rain and evaporation. Closed systems just recycle their input and output and nothing really changes.

The human equivalent of a closed system is a small community in an agrarian society, dominant in preindustrial times and still sometimes present today in communities like those of the Amish or other sects who choose to live apart from society. The material capital of such a community is taken from the earth and turned into recyclable things needed by the population—food, clothing, tools, and the like. The spiritual capital of the community is drawn from its unchanging belief system and embedded as social capital in the community through tradition. Such communities do not evolve, and they are closed to the outside world.

The second state a natural and living system can be in is a steady state. If the glass vase has its cork removed, or the pond has a small stream flowing out of it, the system is now somewhat open to the environment. It will need a steady input to balance its steady output. The stream flowing out of the pond will in turn carve out some banks for itself, but these will remain pretty much the same over the years. The steady-state system has some movement and some inward and outward flow, but it is in balance. Everything in the system is balanced and predictable.

The human equivalent of a steady-state system is a traditional society like Nepal was in the year 2000, before the events that made things begin to unravel there. Some Nepalis traveled outside the system, and some tourists came in. Some material needs were imported, and some products exported. An ethnically mixed population drew on the spiritual capital of several belief systems, but these were long-held, nonproselytizing, and unchanging beliefs, and they managed to live amicably side by side. The community's spiritual capital was invested in social capital represented by strong social and cultural traditions that guided the lives of the vast majority of people, while allowing a few artists and writers to be creative within the familiar boundaries of tradition. In both the closed system and the steady-state system, the spiritual capital of the system is static and passive. It has been received from elders or the culture at large rather than being created by spiritual intelligence.

The "traditional family" and those "family values" that conservative public figures often long for us to return to are ideals of a steady-state system in balance, where there is some inward and outward flow but relationships, roles, and behavior remain traditional and largely predictable. Adam Smith and the early capitalist thinkers modeled their ideas of a free market economy on the steady state, but change is now too rapid for this model to apply.

Nepal, and other such traditional societies, have remained in a state of equilibrium for centuries or even millennia, but modernity is pressing in on them and most—Nepal not least among them—show signs of movement toward one of the two last states that a system can get into: turbulence or self-organizing complexity.

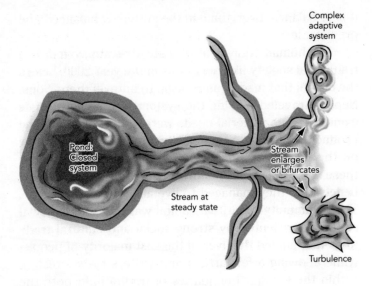

Figure 11.1 *Progression of States in a Natural System*

A stream flowing toward the sea is an open system in a steady state, but because of its openness it can meet conditions that disturb its equilibrium. Other streams join it, to increase the flow and jointly become a river. Sometimes the river meets obstructions—the banks are too narrow for the current flow, or rocks or pieces of wood block the water. The river can no longer remain in a steady state. As illustrated in Figure 11.1, sometimes it now breaks into turbulence (chaos, white water), sometimes into whirlpools. Both are states far from equilibrium (stability).

Turbulence is just turbulence, and there is little we can do with it. It signifies a system that has disintegrated. We all know what it looks like in water. The human equivalent is a state of anarchy.

The whirlpools that form in rivers when their flow increases are one of nature's simplest complex adaptive systems. They have a steady input of material and energy that gets self-organized into a persisting pattern poised far from equilibrium (at *the edge* of chaos). The material (water molecules) and energy constantly flow through the pattern, but the pattern holds its slowly evolving form. Figure 11.2 illustrates a similar complex adaptive system that is creative and constantly adapting to an open future, made up of the forces of society and culture.

The human equivalent of a complex adaptive system is any open, modern democratic society with an externally free capitalist economy. In such open societies and economies, the material capital flowing into the system is still natural resources, augmented by human intelligence and information. The society's social capital is its essentially persisting but constantly evolving structure—its relationships, customs, mores, institutions, and the like. But the system's spiritual capital must now flow from an active spiritual intelligence that can constantly rearticulate abiding values and purposes or create new values and purposes. This can arise only from a critical mass of individuals in the society constantly re-creating themselves and being strong enough to live at the edge of chaos. A more static, passive spiritual capital based on fixed, inherited belief systems could not supply the creative energy flow that such systems require to maintain themselves so far from equilibrium. A complex adaptive system with no input of spiritual capital, or with exhausted spiritual capital, will disintegrate. That is, it will break into turbulence, or anarchy. This has happened at least once before in human history.

The Roman Empire is widely judged to have failed because its spiritual capital (spiritual driving force)

Material capital   Spiritual capital

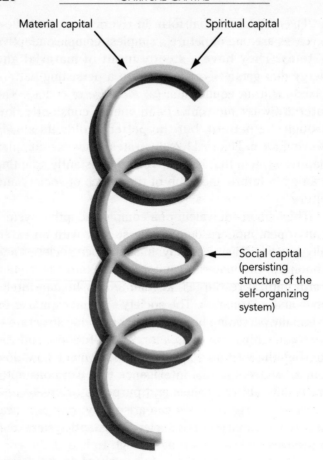

Social capital
(persisting
structure of the
self-organizing
system)

Figure 11.2 *Spiritual Capital: Vital Ingredient for Sustainable System*

became exhausted. The gods of the institutionalized Roman religions were threatened by rising Christianity. The citizens of Rome lost touch with deeper values and purposes, giving themselves over to a lifetime of "bread and circuses." Men could no longer bother to join the empire's army, and barbarians were employed as mercenaries to fight Rome's battles. The barbarians eventually took over and the empire disintegrated. In his *Study of History,* the great British historian Arnold Toynbee traced the rise and fall of twenty such civilizations, in each case attributing their disintegration to an exhaustion of their spiritual vision (that is, exhaustion of spiritual capital).[2]

The Phase Change of Early Capitalism

When a system moves from one state to another, scientists call it a *phase change.* A simple such phase change is when water turns into ice or steam. When a human system moves from a steady state at equilibrium (a traditional society) to a complex adaptive state poised far from equilibrium (a modern society), this, too, is a phase change. I believe that the rise of capitalism in the eighteenth century, coupled with the Industrial Revolution, was such a phase change and that the complex adaptive system thereby created persisted until the twentieth century.

Early capitalism's phase change was powered by the rush of energy pumped into society by the scientific revolution and the rise of Protestantism, though of course it spread to Catholic countries as well.[3] The steady river of Medieval society could no longer hold its banks. New material capital was driven into the system by the Industrial Revolution, new spiritual capital by the spread of a dynamic and work-centered Protestantism, and new social capital grew as the institutions of Enlightenment democracy flourished. America was born, and Europe modernized. The combination produced a complex self-organizing society, always poised at the edge of chaos, but generating unparalleled wealth and creativity for two centuries.

The twentieth century saw increasing chaos and instability—the two world wars, the sapping of Enlightenment ideals, the slow disappearance of Christianity from most people's lives and of its values from society as a whole, the disintegration of families, communities, and relationships, the rise of greed, materialism, and selfishness, the information revolution, globalization, and the diminution of the nation state. It was in this century that capitalism became a self-consuming monster, exhausting its own social and spiritual capital. As we enter the twenty-first century, we even see the potential exhaustion of capitalism's material capital. At this point, Western society's "flow" has reached another bifurcation point. The banks of the river no longer hold. In the inevitable phase change, we can spin off into disintegrating turbulence, or we can become a new complex adaptive system.

This cheekily brief romp through the past century brings me full circle in the book. If we are again to have sustainable capitalism, functioning as a new complex adaptive system, we must use our spiritual intelligence to access fundamental human meanings and values and to give them new life in a recreated form. A critical mass of us, the roughly 15 percent knights and masters who can live at the edge of chaos, will channel new energy (spiritual capital) into a new vortex of evolving, self-organizing structures and relationships that will form the new social capital of our future. In our organizations, the flow of energy through the structures of this system will look something like Figure 11.3.

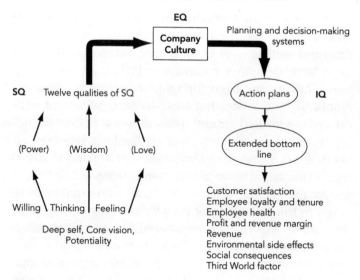

Figure 11.3   *The Organizational Flow Model*

What Can "I" Do?

Just as I was finishing this book, I had lunch with a senior human resources executive, a woman from a major Swiss bank. We spoke about spiritual intelligence and spiritual capital, and she described how she had sought to use and build these in her private life. To develop her own inner life she was practicing yoga, chi gong, and meditation on a regular basis. She read thought-provoking books and listened to good music. She was not religious, but she had high ideals and a strong sense that she wanted her life to make a difference.

"But what can I do?" she pleaded. "What can I do to make the world a better place? Should I change my job and work with an aid agency in Africa?" I told her the story of Peter K., a man who had attended one of my spiritual intelligence workshops.

Peter was an Anglo-Indian in his early forties. He was married, had two teenage children, a son and a daughter, and worked as the senior purchasing manager for a large computer company in Britain. He described himself as having been "uptight," reluctant to show his emotions, and somewhat irascible and impatient with his colleagues and subordinates at work. Before attending the seminar, he had never particularly reflected on his deepest values and aspirations, preferring to avoid topics that might leave him uncomfortable.

As part of the seminar work, all participants were asked to think about what they valued most in life, what they would like to be remembered for, and what difference they would like to make in their own world if they could. We studied and discussed the twelve transformational principles of spiritual intelligence, and at the end of the seminar I asked each person to choose two or three of these principles to make two personal pledges: a change in behavior that to make at home, and a change in behavior to take into their working lives. The group was scheduled to meet again for a follow-up session six weeks later.

When we gathered for the follow-up, Peter was anxious to talk about his pledges and their effect. He said he had decided that he had to become more vision and value led by trying to live more in terms of what he deeply valued. He felt that his life had been lacking in compassion and in spontaneity. These three principles had formed the basis for selecting his two pledges.

At home, Peter decided to talk to his sixteen-year-old son. He and the boy had had a strained relationship, and Peter had just let this go leaving the boy to spend most of his time alone in his bedroom. "I didn't feel that I knew my son, nor that he knew me," he said. After taking his home vow, Peter went to his son's room, spoke openly and frankly about how their distance bothered him, confessed that he hadn't made all the effort he could, and spent an hour or two discussing his son's current interests. The two ended embracing and telling each other of their mutual love. This meeting improved Peter's relationship with his son, and brought added energy to the family as a whole.

At work, Peter vowed to be more patient, to show more of his feelings, and to become a better listener. "I wanted people who worked with me to feel more relaxed and more free to express their diverse opinions. I wanted them to feel free to be more spontaneous around me." To make this new work posture more likely, Peter committed himself to ten minutes of meditation at the end of each working day. Six weeks later, he said that his wife found him more at peace with himself and much easier to live with at home. Colleagues at work described him as a changed person with whom it was much easier to be themselves.

In six short weeks, simply by beginning with an honest assessment of what he really valued in life (family and relationships), Peter had become a knight on a small scale. His willingness to make pledges about how to live these values had led him to bring some energy of spiritual capital into both his home and his workplace. He was not in a position to change the whole direction of his company, but by changing himself he had changed the lives of several people close to him. If these people "pass it forward," they may achieve that critical mass necessary to change the organization within which they work.

So I return here, at the end, to where I began, with the thought from Jung that inspired this book: "In our most private and subjective lives we are not only the passive witnesses of our age, its sufferers, but also its makers. We make our own epoch." To live our lives on the scale of epoch making, it is not necessary to be president of the United States, CEO of a vast global enterprise, or even an aid worker in Africa. We just have to stay true to our own deepest ideals and values and make what difference we can, at whatever level we operate in life. These words from Mother Teresa—which I found in an old and obscure Nepali educational newsletter—may inspire us along the way.

> People are often unreasonable, illogical and
> self-centred. Forgive them anyway.
> If you are kind, people may accuse you of selfish
> ulterior motives. Be kind anyway.
> If you are successful, you will win some false friends
> and some true enemies. Succeed anyway.
> If you are honest and frank, people may cheat you.
> Be honest and frank anyway.
> What you spend years building,
> someone may destroy overnight. Build anyway.
> If you find serenity and happiness,
> people may be jealous. Be happy anyway.
> The good you do today, people will
> often forget tomorrow. Do good anyway.
> Give the world the best you have, and it may never
> be enough. But give the world the best you have anyway.
> You see, in the final analysis, it is all between you
> and God; it was never between you and them anyway.
> —*Mother Teresa*

Notes

Preface
1. Carl Jung, *The Meaning of Psychology for Modern Man.*
2. Ogden Nash, "Don't Grin, or You'll Have to Bear It."

Introduction
1. Francis Fukuyama, *Trust,* p. 26.

Chapter 1
1. Ted Hughes, *Tales from Ovid,* p. 94.
2. Charles Handy, *The Empty Raincoat,* p. 65.
3. Stephen Overell, *Financial Times,* Jan. 9, 2001, p. 18.
4. John Hunt, *Financial Times,* Sept. 27, 2000, p. 24.
5. Frederick Herzberg, Bernard Mausner, and Barbara Block Snyderman, *The Motivation to Work.*
6. Terrence Deacon, *The Symbolic Species.*
7. Viktor Frankl, *Man's Search for Meaning.*
8. Peter Evans, "Model Behaviour," *Oxford Today,* pp. 16–17.

Chapter 2
1. The account of Merck's accomplishments is drawn from David Bollier's *Aiming Higher,* 1997.
2. Janine Nahapiet and Sumantra Ghoshal, "Social Capital, Intellectual Capital, and the Organizational Advantage."

3. Lynda Gratton, *Living Strategy,* p. 7.
4. James Collins and Jerry Porras, *Built to Last,* p. 4.

Chapter 3
1. Hazel Guest and Ian Marshall, "The Scale of Responses, Emotions and Mood in Context."
2. Daniel Goleman, *Emotional Intelligence.*
3. David Hawkins, *Power Vs. Force.*

Chapter 4
1. David Hawkins, *Power Vs. Force,* p. 76.
2. Hawkins, *Power Vs. Force,* p. 82.
3. See M. Csikszentmihalyi, *Living Well.*

Chapter 5
1. Daniel Goleman, *Emotional Intelligence.*
2. Danah Zohar and Ian Marshall, *SQ: Spiritual Intelligence, The Ultimate Intelligence.*
3. Sogyal Rinpoche, *The Tibetan Book of Living and Dying,* p. 40.
4. James Carse, *Finite and Infinite Games.*
5. Terrance Deacon, *The Symbolic Species.*
6. See, for example, M. A. Persinger, "Feelings of Past Lives as Expected Perturbations Within the Neurocognitive Processes That Generate a Sense of Self," and V. S. Ramachandran and Sandra Blakeslee, *Phantoms in the Brain.*
7. See Wolf Singer, "Striving for Coherence."
8. Francis Crick, *The Astonishing Hypothesis,* p. 3.
9. E. Bruce Taub-Bynum, *The Family Unconscious.*
10. Taub-Bynum, *The Family Unconscious,* p. 12.
11. See Danah Zohar, *The Quantum Self;* Roger Penrose, *The Emperor's New Mind;* David R. Hawkins, *Power Vs. Force;* and Lynne McTaggart, *The Field.*
12. See the Global Consciousness Project Web page, http://noosphere.princeton.edu/. Access date, August 13, 2003.

Chapter 7

1. Daniel Goleman, *Emotional Intelligence*.
2. Y. Shoda, M. Mischell, and P. K. Peake, "Predicting Adolescent Cognitive and Self-Regulatory Competencies from Pre-School Delay of Gratification."
3. Charles Handy, *The Alchemists*.
4. Richard Sennett, *The Corrosion of Character*, p. 133.
5. James C. Collins, "Level 5 Leadership."

Chapter 10

1. The quote that opens this chapter comes from St. Bernard's "Sermon of Exhortations for the Knights Templar," as published in James Wasserman's book, *The Templars and the Assassins*, p. 278.
2. See Wasserman, *The Templars and the Assassins*.
3. B. Greyson, "Near-Death Experiences."
4. From Nietzsche's *Thus Spoke Zarathustra*.
5. *The Spiritual Teachings of Ramana Maharshi*, p. 19.

Chapter 11

1. See M. Mitchell Waldrop, *Complexity;* and John Briggs and F. David Peat, *Turbulent Mirror*.
2. Arnold J. Toynbee, *A Study of History*.
3. See, for instance, Max Weber, *The Protestant Ethic and the Spirit of Capitalism*.

Bibliography

Barrett, Richard. *Liberating the Corporate Soul.* Boston: Butterworth/Heinemann, 1998.

Bollier, David. *Aiming Higher.* New York: AMACOM, 1997.

Briggs, John, and F. David Peat. *Turbulent Mirror.* New York: HarperCollins, 1990.

Carse, James. *Finite and Infinite Games.* New York: Ballantine Books, 1986.

Cattell, Raymond B. *Personality and Motivation Structure and Measurement.* Yonkers-on-Hudson, New York: World Book Company, 1957.

Collins, James C. "Level 5 Leadership: The Triumph of Humility and Fierce Resolve," *Harvard Business Review* (January 2001): 66–76.

Collins, James C., and Jerry I. Porras. *Built to Last.* New York: HarperBusiness, 1994.

Crick, Francis. *The Astonishing Hypothesis.* New York: Simon & Schuster, 1994.

Csikszentmihalyi, M. *Living Well.* London: Orion, 1998.

Deacon, Terrance. *The Symbolic Species.* London: Penguin Press, 1997.

Dunn, John. *The Cunning of Unreason.* London: HarperCollins, 2000.

Evans, Peter. "Model Behaviour." *Oxford Today* 13, no. 3 (2001): 16–17.

Frankl, Viktor. *Man's Search for Meaning.* New York: Pocket Books, 1985.

Fukuyama, Francis. *Trust.* New York: Penguin Books, 1995.

Goleman, Daniel. *Emotional Intelligence.* New York: Bantam Books, 1996.

Gratton, Lynda. *Living Strategy.* London: Prentice Hall, 2000.

Greyson, B. "Near-Death Experiences," in *Varieties of Anomalous Experience,* edited by E. Cardena, S. J. Lynn, and S. Krippner. Washington, D.C.: American Psychological Association, 2000.

Guest, Hazel, and Ian Marshall. "The Scale of Responses, Emotions and Mood in Context." *International Journal of Psychotherapy* 2, no. 2 (1997): 149–169.

Handy, Charles. *The Empty Raincoat.* London: Hutchinson, 1994.

———. *The Alchemists.* London: Hutchinson, 1999.

Hawkins, David R. *Power Vs. Force.* Sydney: Hay House, 1995.

Herzberg, Frederick, Bernard Mausner, and Barbara Block Snyderman. *The Motivation to Work,* 2nd ed. New York: Wiley, 1966.

Hughes, Ted. *Tales from Ovid.* London: Faber & Faber, 1997.

Hunt, John. *Financial Times.* Sept. 27, 2000, p. 24.

Isaacs, William. *Dialogue and the Art of Thinking Together.* New York: Currency/Doubleday, 1999.

Jung, C. G. "The Meaning of Psychology for Modern Man," in *The Collected Works of C. G. Jung,* Vol. 10: *Civilization in Transition.* London: Routledge & Kegan Paul, 1953.

Kauffman, Stuart A. *The Origins of Order.* Oxford, England: Oxford University Press, 1993.

McTaggart, Lynne. *The Field.* London: HarperCollins, 2001.

Maharshi, Ramana. *The Spiritual Teachings of Ramana Maharshi.* London: Shambhala, 1972.

Nahapiet, Janine, and Sumantra Ghoshal. "Social Capital, Intellectual Capital, and the Organizational Advantage," in *Knowledge and Social Capital,* edited by Eric L. Lesser. Boston: Butterworth/Heinemann, 2000.

Nash, Ogden. "Don't Grin, or You'll Have to Bear It." In *The Ogden Nash Pocket Book*. Montreal: Pocket Books of Canada, 1944.

Nietzsche, Friedrich. *Thus Spoke Zarathustra*. Translated by R. J. Hollingdale. London: Penguin Classics, 1961. (Originally published 1883–92.)

Overell, Stephen. *Financial Times*. Jan. 9, 2001, p. 18.

Penrose, Roger. *The Emperor's New Mind*. Oxford, England: Oxford University Press, 1989.

Persinger, M. A. "Feelings of Past Lives as Expected Perturbations Within the Neurocognitive Processes That Generate a Sense of Self: Contributions from Limbic Lability and Vectorial Hemisphericity," *Perceptual and Motor Skills,* 83, no. 3, pt. 2 (December 1996): 1107–1121.

Plender, John. *Going Off the Rails*. New York: Wiley, 2003.

Ramachandran, V. S., and Sandra Blakeslee. *Phantoms in the Brain*. London: Fourth Estate, 1998.

Rinpoche, Sogyal. *The Tibetan Book of Living and Dying*. London: Rider, 1992.

Schwartz, Peter. *The Art of the Long View*. New York: Currency/Doubleday, 1991.

Senge, Peter. *The Fifth Discipline: The Art and Practice of the Learning Organization*. New York: Doubleday, 1990.

Sennett, Richard. *The Corrosion of Character*. New York: Norton, 1998.

Shoda, Y., M. Mischell, and P. K. Peake. "Predicting Adolescent Cognitive and Self-Regulatory Competencies from Pre-School Delay of Gratification." *Developmental Psychology* 26 (1990): 978–986.

Singer, Wolf. "Striving for Coherence," *Nature* 397 (4 February 1999): 391–393.

Smith, Simon. *Inner Leadership*. London: Brealey, 2000.

Taub-Bynum, E. Bruce. *The Family Unconscious*. Wheaton, Ill.: Theosophical Publishing House, 1984.

Toynbee, Arnold, J. *A Study of History*. London: Oxford University Press, 1947.

Waldrop, M. Mitchell. *Complexity*. London: Penguin, 1994.

Wasserman, James. *The Templars and the Assassins: The Militia of Heaven.* Rochester, Vt.: Inner Traditions, 2001.

Weber, Max. *The Protestant Ethic and the Spirit of Capitalism.* Translated by Talcott Parsons. London: Routledge Classics, 2001. (Originally published 1920.)

Zohar, Danah. *The Quantum Self.* London: Morrow, 1990.

———. *Rewiring the Corporate Brain.* San Francisco: Berrett-Koehler, 1997.

Zohar, Danah, and Ian Marshall. *SQ: Spiritual Intelligence, The Ultimate Intelligence.* London: Bloomsbury, 2000.

Index

235

About the Authors

DANAH ZOHAR is a physicist, philosopher, and management thought leader who speaks at international conferences on business, education, and leadership. She has made in-house presentations at numerous organizations, including Volvo, Shell, British Telecom, Motorola, Phillips, Skandia Insurance, UNESCO, The Young President's Organization, The European Cultural Foundation, and many others. She is the author or co-author of several books, including *Spiritual Intelligence, Rewiring the Corporate Brain, The Quantum Self, The Quantum Society,* and *Who's Afraid of Schrodinger's Cat?*

IAN MARSHALL is a Jungian-oriented psychiatrist and psychotherapist and the co-author (with Danah Zohar) of *Spiritual Intelligence, The Quantum Society,* and *Who's Afraid of Schrodinger's Cat?* He studied philosophy and psychology at Oxford University before entering medical school at London University. He conducts workshops internationally with Danah Zohar.